SECURITY OFFICER'S
M A N U A L

Bill Clede

LAKELAND PUBLISHING

Cover photograph by Bill Clede.
Photographs by the author unless otherwise credited.
Cover and interior design by Kirstie Larsen.

Published by:
Lakeland Publishing
Lakeland Associates, Inc.
P.O. Box 1010
Minocqua, WI 54548

ISBN 0-9630016-1-2

Library of Congress Catalog Card Number 92-85104

10 9 8 7 6 5 4 3 2 1

First Edition

Printed in the United States of America.

TABLE OF CONTENTS

FOREWORD

Today's society demands that the epidemic of crime be stemmed and the basic security needs of its communities be met. Law enforcement budgets are already feeling the pressures of economic downturns and budget reductions. More and more traditional law enforcement activities are being absorbed by private security organizations. Their functions are to provide the security, safety, and services that law enforcement agencies are unable to extend.

With this expanded role for security comes the need for increased professional training, expertise and ability. No longer can the "watchman" or "rent-a-cop" perform the duties that a professional security officer is expected to carry out.

The role of "Security Officer" and "Police Officer" have never before been so similar. The black and white distinctions of yesteryear are now a continuum of grays. Lines of distinction are drawn more as the exception than the rule.

Today's security officer cannot be the untrained individual epitomized by the stereotype of the "Square Badge" retiree. He or she must be a professional whose training, education, and skill level are consistent with the complex functions and duties they are required to perform.

The security officer of today is as likely to be working with sophisticated electronic detection equipment, computers and communications as performing clock rounds. The skills required surpass those of many other occupations in variety and complexity. This requires training in such diverse areas as physical and electronic security, people skills, CPR, first aid, defensive tactics, report writing, civil and criminal law, and survival skills.

The professional security officer must also be trained in traditional police procedures. The actions—or results of those actions—may end up in the hands of the police. The officer must plan any actions to insure that they comply with federal, state, and local laws, as well as insuring that the initial response assists the police, should they be called.

The security officer is often the first responder to a crime. The officer's actions, or inactions, can dramatically affect the disposition of an incident. If the officer's first response destroys evidence, impedes the investigation, or otherwise interferes in the successful apprehension and prosecution of the perpetrator, everyone loses—the community, the employer, the profession, and ultimately society.

This manual should be required reading for everyone entering this dynamic field. It provides an in-depth analysis of the responsibilities and services that are inherent in the field. The veteran will value this manual because of its thoughtful, thorough review and update of a field which is in a constant state of flux and transition. It provides a thorough analysis of the broad and technical duties that an officer may be requested to perform. It gives a practical interpretation of the technical and social aspects of this complex position.

An individual who has acquired the knowledge, skills and training outlined in this manual will undoubtedly be well equipped to carry out the assigned duties in this exciting field.

—Harry C. Kinne III, Director of Public Safety,
Wesleyan University, Middletown, Connecticut

PUBLISHER'S NOTE

Security officers follow a profession that may put them at risk. Their job is to serve their employer, to protect assets and company services as well as personnel, and enforce company rules with judicious discretion. To accomplish these purposes, the security officer may be required to detain an offender for police, prevent bodily harm by controlling an aggressor, even defend against an attack of deadly force.

This book is intended to provide you with an understanding of the profession, introduce you to the skills you'll need to perform your job, and to show options you may use to fulfill your responsibilities. It is NOT a substitute for training.

Security officers must be trained in the company policies and procedures of their employers, and in the laws and practices applicable to their jurisdictions. Learning psychomotor skills requires hands-on training by a qualified instructor. The proper application of forceful techniques or tools must be justified under the law as it applies to that jurisdiction. Misapplication or misuse of any law, technique, or tools, whether discussed here or not, may make an officer vulnerable to a lawsuit.

The publisher, consultants, and author accept no liability of any sort for any personal injury or property damage that might result from the use or misuse of any of the information, techniques, or applications presented or implied in this book.

ACKNOWLEDGMENTS

The function of a security officer ranges from "tour guide" to "assault force," depending on the mission, and differs according to local and state law. Many have helped to ensure that the information in this book is as complete, accurate, and pertinent as it can be at the time it was written. Many are credited throughout the text, but some are due special thanks.

Roland Ouellette, R.E.B. Security Training, Avon, Connecticut, who reviewed the manuscript and suggested changes.
Harry C. Kinne III, Director of Public Safety, Wesleyan University, Middletown, Connecticut, who suggested many improvements to the manuscript.

And R.E.B. Security instructors:
Les Williams, formerly with the Connecticut State Police Academy, now an independent training consultant.
Larry Koski, former Connecticut State Police, coordinator of Criminal Justice and Public Safety Programs, Mattituck Community College, Waterbury, Connecticut.
Art Gold, Director of Security and Fire Marshall, Mount Sinai Hospital, Hartford, Connecticut.
John O'Hara, formerly with the Connecticut State Police Academy, now Security Director at Mitchell College, New London, Connecticut.
Richard Ballantyne, Chief of Security at Mystic Seaport, Mystic, Connecticut.

Also:
John H. Hickey, Security Site Manager for Connecticut National Bank, Hartford, Connecticut, a Shawmut National Company, who included me in the Certified Officer Training Program conducted for his men.
Fred Jones, Supervisor of Plant Protective Services, Pratt & Whitney Aircraft, Middletown, Connecticut.
Leonard Revoir, Director of Administrative Support Services, New Britain General Hospital, New Britain, Connecticut. He is director of Safety and Security for the hospital.
Officer Timothy M. Dees, Bailiff, Municipal Court, Reno, Nevada.

And the following who reviewed drafts of applicable chapters:
Charles J. Fuhrman, Fuhrman Investigations, Inc., Phoenix, Arizona.
Stuart M. Mulne, Youngstown Security Patrol, Inc., Youngstown, Ohio.

INTRODUCTION

When Neanderthal men retired for the night, I'll bet they posted a guard at the mouth of the cave. You might call that guard the world's first security officer. It wasn't until the passage of the Metropolitan Police Act of 1829 in England that an organized police force came into being. Before that time, the London metropolis had its Day Patrol, Night Patrol, and Horse Patrol. Sir Robert Peel, then Home Secretary, defined the structure for what is today's Scotland Yard. This was the beginning of an organized police force, empowered by law to prevent and detect crime and apprehend offenders.

In medieval Europe, knights provided security for lords and ladies. In the Colonies, every able-bodied male citizen had to stand Citizen's Night Watch. Our Founding Fathers did not enact our Constitution until it was agreed to add a Bill of Rights. The Second Amendment states, "A well-regulated militia being necessary to the security of a free state, the right of the people to keep and bear arms shall not be infringed." Male citizens were expected to answer the "call to arms," bringing with them the arms needed for the job.

Allen Pinkerton became the first law enforcement officer hired to protect the private interests of the railroad in 1855. It was in the private sector that the first SWAT unit was formed. A group of railroad special agents were formed into the Rangers in 1899. The Rangers acquired a specially equipped baggage car which carried eight men and their horses. The car could be rushed to the scene of a train robbery, where the Rangers mounted up and pursued the robbers on horseback. Edwin Holmes built the first central alarm system in 1858. ADT, American District Telegraph Company, was formed in 1874. Washington Brink set up Brink's armored car service in 1891, and William Burns founded his international detective agency in 1909.

Even today, there are just two significant differences between what we call a police officer and a security officer: the power of arrest, and who pays the salary. In some states, a security officer has a "citizen's arrest" power. Or, for example, a security officer may hold a special police commission. A state hospital complex in my area recently changed its law enforcement unit from a full-powered police department to a limited-powered security division, but the state still pays the salaries.

It took police many years to outgrow the epithet of "flatfoot." Likewise, it is taking a long time for security to outgrow the idea of "night watchman." Those who know tell me that the image of private security stands today about where the police image stood 20 years ago.

Times are changing. Private security is one of the fastest growing industries today. There are an estimated 1.5 million people employed in private security and the number is growing every day. There are some 622,000 sworn police officers, and the number has not grown over the past 20 years. Government can no longer afford to increase expenditures of tax dollars on law enforcement. In 1986, private protection services spent $22 billion. Police budgets added up to $13 billion.

Consider the purposes of law enforcement beyond the motto "To Protect and to Serve." A police officer is trained to maintain order, prevent crime, detect an offense, detain the perpetrator, and report all the facts and circumstances so the case can be properly handled by court authorities. Doesn't the security officer do the same? Of course. In addition, a police officer may take an offender into custody and present the subject before court officials. The security officer may also detain an offender to be presented to police when circumstances warrant. While the security officer usually does not have a police officer's power of arrest, the effect is the same.

There is little practical difference between security and police. Each is hired to enforce a particular set of rules. As there are different kinds of police officers to enforce different bodies of law depending on the needs of a jurisdiction, there are also different kinds of security officers depending on the needs of their employers.

There is no longer a fine line of demarcation between security and police. Many states passed laws making railroad officers police, with powers of arrest. Some universities have security forces, some have police forces. But the job each of these forces performs is essentially the same. A resident state trooper in my state checked a gun store on routine patrol. He interrupted a burglary in progress and was killed in the fusillade of fire before he even got his car stopped. Two security officers in an armored car were delivering money to a small bank when two criminals approached from behind and opened fire, killing one. The second officer shot back and killed one of the bandits. Similar situations, both were ambushed by armed criminals, yet one was a police officer and the other a private security officer. Both are just as dead.

The United States Constitution reserves police power to the states. State law establishes police and is the basis for their powers. But there is also a basis for private security. Citizens have the right to protect their own person or property. When you are employed by a corporate "citizen," the right to protect that property extends to you.

There is another, though diminishing, difference between police and private security officers. Because training requirements for police officers came first, and have grown over the years, a "real cop" takes pride in the accomplishment of qualifying for a badge. Some states are now requiring certification and training for "rent-a-cops." Earning this certification will offer the private security officer the same pride when qualifying for a badge.

The only real difference between public law enforcement and private security is in how the two jobs are perceived. If you study, seek training, develop professional skills, and conduct yourself as a proud officer, the professional attitude will be reflected in your job performance. If you consider yourself a positive influence, you will be perceived that way by others. This is true for either a security or police officer.

Security is becoming an adjunct to, and an extension of, public law enforcement. Government pays police officers with tax dollars to provide security in the public jurisdiction. Corporations pay security officers with company funds to provide security in their private jurisdictions. Private security picks up where public police leaves off. An officer with the Las Vegas Metro Police tells me his department could never handle the demands for service if it weren't for the casino security forces. He said that if those security forces were an organized police department, it would be the fourth largest in the state.

In June 1991, Sen. Al Gore (D-TN) introduced legislation in

the U.S. Congress to establish guidelines and training programs for security officers. Ten states have no statutes at all, and the others are a patchwork of uneven and often ineffective laws. The Security Officer Employment Standards Act of 1991 aims to set uniform guidelines to help states ensure that private security forces receive adequate screening and training. While this bill would affect only security officers in federal employment, or employed by a government contractor, it would set up a grant program to help states set their own standards.

Because of these upcoming requirements, this book alone cannot give you a qualification as Certified Security Officer. This book's purpose is to present you with an understanding of, and appreciation for, the job of security officer and the skills required to perform the job successfully. Armed with a better understanding of what is involved, you will get more out of training and retain the information longer.

This is a fluid field. Techniques constantly improve, laws change, new technology develops. For these reasons, I urge you to write me in care of the publisher. Suggest new and better ways of doing the job. Perhaps you've developed a unique solution that other officers should know about. Later editions of this book will include this input and credit the sources. Both individual officers and the profession will benefit.

—Bill Clede

Chapter 1
WHAT MAKES A GOOD SECURITY OFFICER?

There is little practical difference between a police officer and a security officer. But that word "practical" is significant. Police officers must complete rigorous training and meet requirements for continuing in-service training. To a lesser degree this is true for security officers as more states require training for certification.

The security officer is the visitor's first impression of a company. The officer needs a basic education to interact successfully with people. The officer also needs advanced study in the specialized field of security. A profession is "An occupation or vocation requiring training in the liberal arts or the sciences and advanced study in a specialized field." Therefore, private security is a profession, and *security officer* is a title that must be earned.

ATTITUDES

A company's attitude is critical to the professional standing of its security department. An employer does not expect you to be "the police," but too many don't really know what to expect of security. The company doesn't want to be exposed to liability. Yet, you are expected to enforce company rules. You should know your company's attitude regarding prosecution of offenders before you call the police. If the company has declined to prosecute in the past, then you can understand that police response will be limited.

You need to develop a relationship with local police that promotes mutual assistance. Do not expect police to corral offenders just to help you recover property. That's not their job. While the recovery of property and prevention of injuries are

Security for an industrial complex begins at the front gate.

both important issues, there are other aspects of a situation which may or may not lead to prosecution. Many suspects are verbally abusive or threatening. A police presence may help to avoid what might become a bad situation.

You are two steps down the path to professionalism when your employer publishes reasonable regulations and empowers well-trained officers to enforce them. However, the employer may not realize that empowering you, yet denying you adequate training, can incur liability.

Here is an example of liability incurred by improper training in the public sector. In *Leite v. City of Providence (1978)*, the court decided that the town, and not just the police officer, could be held liable if the plaintiff's injury resulted from non-existent or grossly inadequate training and supervision of a police department.

Popow v. City of Margate (1979) applied the Leite decision to the type of training provided. Margate's officers received basic training at the state police academy and in-service firearms training on the range every six months. The case concerned the fatal nighttime shooting of an innocent bystander by a police officer in a residential community. Range training provided no instruction in shooting at a moving target, night shooting, shooting in residential areas, or shooting decisions. Evidence was presented that the chief considered the rules of firing in residential streets a matter of common sense, not requiring detailed explanation. The court held the training to be "grossly inadequate" and found for the plaintiff.

The same principles could apply to a private company that sends a security officer out to do a law enforcement job without adequate training. Whatever your employer's training budget, you are judged by what you do and how you act. It's in your own interest to get training on your own if it is not provided by your employer.

Your attitude determines the respect you receive as a security officer. If you act like a professional, others will see you as a professional.

PERSONALITY

It takes a special kind of person to be a security officer. Aside from the ability to endure verbal abuse, you must remain alert during hours of monotonous patrol, yet react quickly when necessary. You must be able to switch instantly from a state of near somnambulism to an adrenaline-filled struggle for survival. You must learn your patrol area thoroughly in order to recognize out-of-the-ordinary activity. You are a part of the business community and the personification of your company. The corporate image is perceived by visitors on the basis of the image you project.

Working with local police will test your professionalism. A police officer described an encounter with a security officer as follows: "A uniformed security officer in a police-type car was parked at about 6 a.m. next to a saltwater intrusion well being drilled. I pulled up and identified a lieutenant of a local security company. The officer was wearing a 6-inch .357 Magnum revolver, about two days growth of beard, and a uniform that he had apparently worn for several days. When I requested he give

As the symbol of authority, the security officer knows where everything is. Officers are often asked for directions.

the station a courtesy contact with information about who will be there and how long, the officer appeared indignant that I questioned him."

The security officer had been hired by the state to guard the well over the weekend. "These people were there four days—but no one contacted the station," according to the police officer. "If private security is going to reach a level of community trust, then it must come from within the security field itself."

It takes initiative, effective judgment, and imagination to cope with complex situations such as family disturbances, potential suicides, robberies in progress, gory accidents, or natural disasters. This all occurs, even inside an office building.

Security officers must be able to size up a situation instantly and react properly, perhaps even making a life or death decision. You need mature judgment to determine whether an offender should be held for police or reported to the boss. You need self-restraint to use only the degree of force justified by the circumstance.

Security officers must possess the confidence and initiative to perform their functions when supervisors are not present. And, when called upon, they must be able to take part in a strike force team under the direct command of a superior. They must take charge in chaotic situations, yet avoid alienating participants or bystanders. They must be a helpful influence when crowds gather, yet single out and placate an agitator trying to cause a riot.

Security officers must have curiosity tempered with tact. They will be called upon to question people, ranging from a traumatized victim to a suspected perpetrator. They must be brave enough to face an armed criminal, cope with the stress of a deadly assault, help a woman deliver a baby, yet remain alert on patrol during the wee hours. They must maintain a balanced perspective when exposed to the worst side of human nature, yet be objective in dealing with the public.

Security officers must be adept at a variety of psychomotor skills: operating a vehicle in normal and emergency situations; using weapons properly under adverse conditions; maintaining agility, endurance, and strength in applying techniques to defend themselves while detaining a suspect with a minimum of force.

Then, when it is all over, the security officer must be able to explain what happened—in writing. The written explanation must communicate events to someone who wasn't there in such a way that there is no opportunity for misunderstanding.

CAREER DEVELOPMENT

The professional development of its officers is a concern of every security company or corporate security department. Many send officers to courses to help them develop into more valuable employees. You may have to argue, cajole, and stubbornly persist in submitting applications, but opportunities are available. Professional development is a key factor in anyone's success, but it won't just come to you. You need to work on it throughout your entire career.

A security trainer told me about a college security officer he came to know well. The officer paid for and attended many of the trainer's courses on his own. The officer paid attention to potential career opportunities, applying for and successfully securing a position as security director at a college in a neighboring state.

IT DEPENDS ON YOU

Few people in today's work force have active professional development agendas. You need to have a future vision. What conditions and requirements will challenge the security field in the future? Projecting that, identify what you must do to fit into the picture.

Know yourself. Recognize your own levels of knowledge and skill, stage of career development, professional and organizational contributions, and the knowledge and skills you want to develop. Ask those who have worked with you to help you assess your abilities.

Know the profession. What are the key professional challenges you will face in the next five years? Who else will be facing these issues or who will have a useful perspective on them? Seek associates who will be helpful in developing your skills. Attending professional association conferences puts you in touch with others with similar interests. You will learn not only from the seminars, but from conversations with peers relaxing next to the swimming pool.

Develop an action plan. Define your goals. Set reasonable short-term objectives. Plan what you need to do to meet those objectives, then review and revise your plan every year.

Develop learning skills. Continually improve your ability to listen, concentrate, read, think, explore ideas openly, and generate innovative ideas. You can learn from a surprising number of sources, but think critically to recognize and control your biases and blind spots.

At one time private security was an entry level position to access a career in police work. It has since become a career field in its own right. Charles Connally, chairman of the American

Society for Industrial Security's (ASIS) Law Enforcement Liaison Council, once told a police audience that some private security forces are way ahead of many police departments in technology and available security resources. Some 200 colleges offer courses, 25 offer BA degrees, ten offer MA degrees, and the University of Michigan has started a doctorate program.

There may be many security departments where you live, with few police departments covering the same region. There are probably more career opportunities in private security than in the police profession. As more companies recognize the importance and value of a professional security force, the career potential will continue to improve.

PROMOTIONS ARE EARNED

Company policies, as well as union contracts, spell out exact procedures for promotions. At promotion time, when all but the top few candidates have been eliminated, how is the final decision made? The subjective opinions of your superiors, passed on as recommendations to the boss, are often the key. Everything you do from day one, beyond your performance on the job, influences those opinions. Do you arrive for work on time? Are you eager to learn? Do you find things to investigate when you're on patrol? Do you seek training on your own?

Many students in security training courses are not sent by their employers. They are conscientious officers who pay their own tuition to get necessary training in the side-handle baton or OC aerosol, for example, that they were issued without adequate training.

A positive, professional job attitude is comprised of the willingness to slosh through a swamp after a suspect, to accept demanding assignments and complete them with professional effectiveness, to back up your partner in the face of danger, to plan a patrol so you're likely to be in the right spot at the right time, and to seek every opportunity to improve.

A security officer's professional performance is the basis for the effectiveness reports that a supervisor writes. The completeness of reports, judgment in exercising the duties of the office, relationships with the community and local police—all of these influence a supervisor's opinion when asked to evaluate a security officer.

Chapter 2
SECURITY TODAY

The "night watch" of early times evolved into a present-day police function of local governments. While the functions of private security are similar to police, the uses of private security are far more diverse. Basic skills are much the same for all who enforce the law or company rules, but the public's police do not patrol private property. The concerns of private security range from white collar crime to terrorism.

CATEGORIES OF SECURITY

Corporate offices, even in downtown buildings, are vulnerable to many kinds of misdeeds. A worker who suspected a supervisor of having an affair with his wife came to work with a gun. In the ensuing scuffle, the supervisor was wounded and went to the hospital. A customer, irate over the handling of an insurance claim, showed up at the office to seek revenge. A female security officer in a corporate downtown office building was brutally murdered during the night. A bank officer went into the attached parking garage after work to get her car. She was found the next day in a nearby park, raped and murdered.

A federal study shows that the leading cause of death of American women in the workplace is murder. From 1980 through 1985, 950 women were killed at their workplaces. That's 41 percent of all job-related deaths for females, according to the National Institute for Occupational Safety and Health. Gunshot wounds accounted for 64 percent, stabbing 19 percent, choking seven percent, and blunt trauma six percent. Most of the victims were in four occupations; sales personnel, clerical, service employees, and supervisors.

Defense plants challenge the security officer with all the

threats listed above, plus the possibility of espionage. A factory that makes military products could be a complex of buildings with different security classifications attached to each. Some may contain secrets critical to national defense, or proprietary secrets that give the company a competitive edge. Government contracts may mandate that security include a specially trained Special Weapons and Tactics (SWAT) unit.

Thousands of workers enter and leave the workplace at every shift change. At one plant where I worked, everyone wore photo ID badges. As a test, we made a simulation of a badge. On close examination it was obviously a fake. A new security officer, unknown to other employees and wearing civilian clothes, wore the false badge throughout the area. Finally, a security supervisor challenged him inside one of our most secure areas and took him into custody.

Nuclear plants are exceptionally secure sites with well-planned fencing and patrols. But, if terrorists want to cripple a plant, they may carry out an armed assault to shut down the power generator. The threat includes the potential use of heavy military weapons. It's a requirement that a nuclear security force be able to defend against a "commando" assault. Such special forces are beyond the scope of this book, but it shows the range of "private security."

Shopping malls are private property. While police may patrol the parking areas, the public's officers do not walk the beats inside—security officers do. However, there is a wide variety in the quality of mall private security jobs. While mall management should provide professional security services, too many appear only to be filling an insurance requirement. One friend of mine in mall security complains, "Office business, such as transferring money from banks and other office errands, have priority over mall patrol. They even send officers off-property when they are the only officers present." But another friend, in a different mall, says "It's the same as walking a foot beat with the police department, except you aren't carrying a gun."

Retail stores, even those in shopping malls, are a different kind of security concern. While the public must have easy access, the company doesn't want people walking out with products they haven't purchased. Stores are responsible for their own security and the larger ones provide internal security. In addition to the usual in-plant concerns, there is the prospect of shoplifting. As my friend said, "You may have trouble finding a sales clerk, but you can be sure that security is watching you through the closed-circuit television cameras."

Transportation is the lifeline of America's economy. The only thing of value that can be moved without transportation from manufacturer to distributor, or distributor to dealer, is money transferred by computer. Even then, bills or stock certificates or bullion must be moved so you can cash your paycheck. Shipments must fit into a schedule. They're vulnerable at many points. Highjacking was a well-established crime long before the advent of airline hijacking.

Hospitals offer unique private security challenges. They are repositories of drugs and targets for the addict on the street. When victims of violence come through the emergency room door, they need medical attention—but is there an irate spouse or rival gang member following the ambulance to finish the job? You never know who will show up, including a mentally disturbed person waiting to pounce on anyone available.

Open to the public 24 hours a day, hospitals have numerous sensitive areas. Controlling access to the institution presents complex problems. Expensive equipment is attractive to thieves, and narcotics and syringes are stored in many areas.

Community housing developments may be beyond the jurisdiction or capabilities of local police. The small police department may not have the resources to provide constant patrol in an exclusive unincorporated community. The community hires its own security patrol to provide full-time police functions in the area. In such community security departments, there is little difference between security and police—except the power of arrest. Sometimes these communities incorporate, become a local government, and their security force becomes a police department.

Executive protection is a specialized and increasingly necessary function which may be required of the security officer. Corporate executives must travel to sensitive areas in other countries. Security paves the way by contacting local authorities and determining the safest routes and hotels. The protective service agent travels with and, at all costs, safeguards the well-being of the executive.

While local police have jurisdiction in this unincorporated community, primary patrol responsiblity belongs to the community's public safety department.

ROLE OF THE SECURITY OFFICER

The security officer's function is to perform for an employer essentially the same tasks that a police officer performs for the public. A study sponsored by the National Institute of Justice (NIJ) concluded that public police and private security should share crime prevention materials, specialized equipment, expertise and personnel. It showed that non-criminal demands on law enforcement have grown while the capacity of police to handle them has not. This is the impetus for the growing demand for private security and protective services. Many minor offenses are now properly handled by private security. Competent security officers can perform a preliminary investigation and determine whether a case should be referred to police. The police get the case with much of the preliminary work completed.

In *Law and Order* magazine, Richard Bocklet tells the story of several organized cooperative efforts:

In mid-1986, the Area Police-Private Security Liaison Program (APPL) was launched in New York City. It linked Midtown, North, South, and 17th Precincts with 30 private security forces in a structured anti-crime effort. Mike McNulty, a former police chief and now vice president for the Rockefeller Center Security Department, explains that the private sector conducts investigations, security audits, and maintains detailed crime records, along with complete files including pedigree and photographs of offenders.

What began as an experiment blossomed into units in Downtown, Uptown, and Downtown Brooklyn APPLs. Police provide private security with information on local crime trends and patterns, wanted persons, lost or stolen property, etc. In turn, private security funnels information to police and acts as "eyes and ears" in places the police don't normally go.

Yes, it took some time before the social barriers were broken. The police academy conducted training for security officers. In-service training for police included the new realities of the private sector professionals and how they help police.

One incident does not make a rule. There are more.

The Dearborn, Michigan Security Network was formed in February 1988 among local businesses and the Dearborn police. Dearborn police and security agencies in the network share crime information through the NIJ Criminal Justice Computer Bulletin Board System (BBS). A grant from Ford Motor Company paid for the computer and modem to access the BBS. A password is required to access the files on armed robbery, fraud and con games, stolen vehicles, financial institution crimes, commercial and residential unlawful entry, and upcoming crime seminars.

Corporal Doug Laurain of the Dearborn Police Department said the BBS pays off. "An insurance company security guard reported a man was stealing from cars in their parking lot," Laurain said. "I added the item to our armed robbery file, alerting other security managers in the area. Sure enough, three days later, the individual was apprehended. The apprehension was directly attributable to the bulletin board information."

"I learned about teenagers breaking into cars from the bulletin board," said Linda Kinczowski, director of safety and

Growing non-criminal demands on law enforcement are the reason for a growing demand for private security and protective services.

security for the University of Michigan at Dearborn. "I distributed the modus operandi (MO) to my staff. They spotted the individuals loitering in our parking lot. When they recognized they were under surveillance, they quickly moved away and haven't been seen since."

The Downtown Detroit Security Executive Council was formed in 1984. It includes 50 organizations, public and private, including the United States Marshals Service, Secret Service, FBI, Detroit Police Department, Wayne County Sheriff's Department, Ford, General Motors, Chrysler, Stroh's, and the Henry Ford Hospital.

There are programs underway in Anne Arundle County in Maryland; Tacoma, Washington; and Dallas, Texas. A Dallas police officer wrote a "Citizen's Certificate of Merit" to a private security agent after he provided aid at a burglary scene.

This emphasis on "police" should not imply that a security officer's only responsibilities are access and crime. They are often the ones who discover an insecure situation, or are first at the scene of a fire.

Your role as a security officer is defined by your employer. A good security manager helps the company to define that role properly.

Chapter 3
BASIC SKILLS

PUBLIC RELATIONS

Security may be a prime responsibility—but the security officer is also a company's public relations representative. Who deals with the public on a more personal basis than the security officer?

Your post may be at a desk in the front lobby where everyone who enters or leaves the premises sees you. You are the first impression—good or bad—that a visitor has of your company. Will visitors see an overweight, unshaven, indifferent slob in a rumpled uniform? Or will they see a physically fit, well-groomed officer in a clean and neatly pressed uniform with shined shoes and belt? It's obvious which of these examples will create the better impression.

Public relations is more than appearance. What if you are reading a magazine, paying no attention to those passing by. Then, someone walks up to ask a question and you respond with "Huh?" You know the impression that creates. Suppose, instead, you are alert and attentive. When you notice someone acting confused, you approach and state, "Hello, I'm Officer Clede. May I help you?" Put yourself in the visitor's place.

The security officer will generally deal with four segments of the public—visitors, employees, news media, and telephone callers.

Visitors are the first of your four publics. Greet visitors with a smile, show a sincere desire to help, courteously log them in and issue badges if required. Be attentive and show patience and tact. Know the answers to the more common questions, such as the name of the company, its business, the names of top executives and department heads, locations of different departments, opening time of offices, and who to call for additional information.

Security officers for the Shawmut National Corporation present a professional image.

While some employees may consider you to be one of them, most will see that you represent management. It's your duty to enforce rules without making enemies. You may have to politely tell an offender to put out a cigarette in a designated "no smoking" area. And you may have to authoritatively tell an employee that company rules forbid entry through a certain door, then offer to relay a message or help in some way.

To be sensitive, yet authoritative, you need to cultivate a military bearing—forceful yet helpful. Your job is to obey the rules and to ensure that others do the same. You can be pleasant, polite, and maintain your professional demeanor without becoming "one of the guys."

Do not apologize for doing your duty. This implies weakness, that you are not comfortable with your authority. Middle management personnel may pick up on that and try to force you to comply with their wishes. An apology may even cause some people to become belligerent.

Another pitfall when dealing with employees is being drawn into an argument. An employee bent on breaking the rules may argue the reason for the rule. "Theirs not to reason why . . .", as was written in the classic poem, *Charge of the Light Brigade.* State the facts with no arguments. Just how assertive you should be in enforcing the rules depends on company policy and the situation.

News media is one of your publics—whether you like it or not. Company policy probably prohibits you from making statements to the press. However, at the scene of a newsworthy event, you may be the only company representative present. In no case should you answer questions about the company or its actions. Know to whom the media should be referred and, if necessary, contact that person.

Telephone callers are an important part of your public. In many cases, security answers the phone during off-business hours. See the section on telephone etiquette.

SECURITY COMMUNICATIONS

Security officers can be involved in a wide range of emotionally charged situations. What you say and how you say it can be critical.

A dispatch center on a college campus is aided by computer. On the wall are alarm panel readouts. Phones and the base station radio are on the right.

"Communication" means conveying information from one person to another. If the receiver understands something different from what you transmitted, that's not communication. Suppose the phone rings and an excited caller yells, "There's an accident, 5th floor accounting, [cough] injuries!" and hangs up. Did the caller say there were no injuries? Multiple injuries? Either way, something did not get communicated. Your response could be correct, or very wrong.

Telephone Techniques
Although reading and writing are taught in school, it is amazing how few people learn to speak properly on the telephone. A caller's impression of your company begins when you answer the phone.

There are three elements to placing or receiving a call: 1) identify yourself, 2) identify your company, and 3) identify the person you wish to speak to or ask how you may help.

27

A two-way radio is your link to headquarters and the means to request help. Keep your dispatcher informed of your location and activities.

Proper identification saves time. "Baybank Security, Officer Clede. How may I help you?" If the call is a wrong number, the caller knows immediately. If not, you sound efficient and courteous. If it's a question you can't answer immediately, ask if the caller would like to wait, or would prefer that someone call back.

Tact wins friends. If another line rings and the call you're on isn't an emergency, excuse yourself and ask if you may put the caller on hold. But return to the original call promptly, and thank the caller for waiting.

If you are calling someone and you know it will be a long call, it is courteous to give warning and ask if another time would be more convenient. If time is critical, say so. "I'm sorry to inconvenience you, but we need this information right away."

Special training is given to those answering emergency lines. Sometimes callers are distraught and you need to calm them before you can get the information you need. Your company may have a form to prompt you with the questions to ask: exact location, any injuries, nature of the problem, and other information to help a responding officer.

Radio Techniques

A two-way radio is your link to headquarters, the means by which you can request help. If you are on motor patrol, keep your dispatcher informed of where you are and what you're doing. When you stop to investigate a suspicious situation, call in your location and the plate numbers of suspicious cars. A good dispatcher will check back if you don't clear the stop within a reasonable time. On your way to a call, your radio is the means by which other officers can give you vital information. It's a good bet that the radio has saved more lives than the gun.

You'll likely develop a verbal "shorthand" to save time and be less intelligible to the thousands of citizens with scanners. For example, you might hear one car call another and say, "Lower level?" That means the officer wants to meet the other for a chat in the remote level of the big shopping center parking lot. But be wary of picking up sloppy habits and imprecise pet phrases. When the chips are down, don't take chances on being understood. Use the procedural words dictated by your department. Speak distinctly. Be precise.

Many police radio procedures use codes. There are many variations of the familiar "10" signals. The purpose of such codes is not secrecy. Listeners can identify a variety of codes simply by listening over time. Their real purpose is to convey a precise meaning in the shortest possible time.

GOOD OPERATING PRACTICE

With the crowded airwaves today, your radio probably uses a squelch circuit that is opened by a sub-audible tone or tone burst. When you pick up the mike, a switch unmutes the receiver so you can listen to the frequency for a few seconds before you begin transmitting. If another officer in a distant location is in the middle of shouting for help, you don't want to activate your nearby transmitter to get a time check. Federal Communications Commission (FCC) rules and regulations require that you monitor the frequency to be sure it is clear before you transmit.

INTERNATIONAL PHONETIC ALPHABET

A—Alpha	N—November
B—Bravo	O—Oscar
C—Charlie	P—Papa
D—Delta	Q—Quebec
E—Echo	R—Romeo
F—Foxtrot	S—Sierra
G—Golf	T—Tango
H—Hotel	U—Uniform
I—India	V—Victor
J—Juliet	W—Whiskey
K—Kilo	X—X-ray
L—Lima	Y—Yankee
M—Mike	Z—Zulu

INTELLIGIBILITY

It's imperative that someone on the other end of the transmission understands what you are saying. Speak d-i-s-t-i-n-c-t-l-y. Practice pronouncing the words you use the most. Officers who mumble often have radio transmissions that are twice as long as they need to be because they have to repeat themselves.

Learn to use terms correctly. "Roger" means "I received and understand your message." It does not mean "yes." "Affirmative" means "yes." Don't ask for a "reiteration," use "say again." "Stand by" means wait for further information, or wait a minute while the dispatcher handles an emergency phone call.

Another bad habit is reaching over to the dashboard, pushing the push-to-talk button, and talking without bringing the mike to your mouth. That may be okay for a quick acknowledgment but not for conveying information. Technicians usually set the mike audio level so a normal voice is barely heard with the mike at arm's length. This helps to subdue the background noise inside your mobile environment, so your voice comes through loud and clear.

Avoid the habit of clicking the mike key a couple of times to acknowledge a transmission, instead of saying "Roger" or "10-4." Do those clicks mean, "Okay," or "Someone's got me by the neck and I can't talk"?

SPELL PHONETICALLY

Spell out unusual words, usually names, to convey them accurately. Is it Steven or Stephen? That could make a difference when you're asking for a license check.

Spelling phonetically can be done efficiently. Don't say, "G as in George, U as in Unit, S as in Sam." It takes less time to say, "Golf Uniform Sierra." The international phonetic alphabet is listed on the opposite page.

There used to be many different phonetic alphabets, and some used words that were difficult to pronounce. The old police phonetic alphabet was one example. Finally, the nations of the world got together and developed a standard list of phonetics most suitable to persons of all ethnic backgrounds and languages. You may hear it used on police frequencies, especially by officers recently out of training.

EMERGENCY MEDICAL

You are the first responder. You are the one sent to find out what's wrong. It could be a fall down the stairs, a heart attack, a bloody accident, or a knife-slashed victim.

Security officers today are trained in basic first aid. There are many excellent texts on first aid. Since specific training is required, it won't be discussed in detail here. However, understanding some of the principles will augment such training.

EMS (EMERGENCY MEDICAL SERVICE) CALL

Remember the ABCs of any medical emergency: check the Airway, check Breathing, and check Circulation. Unless these are functioning, the victim won't survive to benefit from further treatment.

If you are called to aid a choking victim, the Heimlich maneuver may clear the airway. The Heimlich maneuver involves grasping the victim from behind, putting the thumb side of your fist just under the rib cage, and quickly exerting pressure inward and upward against the diaphragm. This causes an explosive expulsion of air that may clear the obstruction.

Cardiopulmonary resuscitation (CPR) should be required training for officers because it can mean survival for a victim suffering cardiac or pulmonary arrest. Basically, CPR provides victims with air and blood circulation until either they revive or the paramedics arrive. It buys time. CPR involves chest compressions to pump blood and forced breathing to provide oxygen. Training and practice teach you how to establish the rhythm necessary to mimic the body function. Anyone can learn it, and should. CPR saves lives.

A well-equipped first aid kit in the cruiser is an important part of your equipment.

TRAUMA CALL

When responding to an accident there is a sequence of actions you must perform quickly. First, after advising the dispatcher of your arrival, evaluate the dangers—downed power lines or escaping gases, for example. Second, determine the number of victims (an explosion could throw some victims clear of the immediate area.) Finally, survey the situation and protect against hazards that might aggravate it.

As you manage the emergency, call the dispatcher to request necessary services. Do you need an ambulance? More than one? If there are no injuries, responses required from other agencies can be more measured. Downed power lines require the attention of the company's electrical department or public utility company. A hazardous material spill requires notification of environmental safety officials.

Then take the time to check all the victims. Your first survey of victims will confirm that each is breathing and to identify the seriously injured. Then return to those who need immediate attention, inventory the injuries, and take remedial action.

You must control serious bleeding to buy time for the victim. Direct pressure with a gauze pad is best. If you add a dressing later, apply it over the old one. You may need to use a pressure point to control bleeding from a specific wound. Perhaps elevating the wound will slow the bleeding. A tourniquet is a last resort. Then treat for shock. Loosen restrictive clothing and warm the victim.

Finally, check for signs which indicate the type of problem. Gray, clammy, ashen skin color indicates shock. Check the pupils of the eyes: if dilated, possible cardiac arrest; if constricted, possible drug use; if unequal, possible brain damage, stroke, or head injury.

Treatment for a stabbing victim is different. The knife may be still sticking out of the chest or back. If so, leave it. Bandage around it, if you must, but never remove a penetrating object.

When treating a gunshot victim you may hear a sucking sound around the chest. The chest is a closed system. If it's penetrated, air may be inhaled through the chest wall rather than the nose. It needs to be closed with a dressing covered by plastic to make it airtight. Make sure that the exit wound, if any, is also sealed.

If you suspect a fracture, stabilize it by splinting a limb or joint in the same position as you find it.

Your job is to take immediate action to prevent further injury and to buy time for the victim until medical responders arrive.

GOOD SAMARITAN LAWS

If your state has a Good Samaritan law, it will protect you to the extent that you act in accordance with your training. These laws protect persons trained in or licensed to practice first aid, CPR, or emergency care from liability for civil damages arising from humanitarian actions. It became necessary when even physicians found themselves the target of litigation. In my state, the law specifically exempts paid or volunteer firemen or policemen from liability for forcible entry into a residence to render emergency first aid. You should check the laws of your state for the specific wording; it may include lifeguards, teachers, ski patrol members, or ambulance personnel.

AIDS

AIDS is an acronym for Acquired Immune Deficiency Syndrome. It is caused by a virus, Human Immunodeficiency Virus (HIV). It ages the body's natural defense system. AIDS is not transmitted by casual contact, but through body fluids, particularly blood and semen. A security officer's contact with a victim is far from casual; the officer bandages a bleeding wound or gives CPR, including mouth-to-mouth resuscitation. Your medical kit should include a plastic airway that prevents direct contact. The usual cuts and bruises on your hands provide a body fluid-to-body fluid route. Even in your normal routine, you might prick your finger on the unseen hypodermic needle during a body search of an infected drug abuser.

There is reason for fear. Recent reports show that health care workers have become infected a year after their skin was splashed with the blood of AIDS patients. Others have been infected on the job by accidentally being stuck with infected needles. Clearly, you should guard against contact with blood, even though the chance of infection is still thought to be remote.

Not all the advice that's been published on AIDS can be followed by security officers in emergency situations, but you should be aware of what the medical experts are saying.

• When in a situation where contact with body fluids is unavoidable, protective garments are advisable.

- Disposable latex gloves should be worn when arresting a potentially violent bleeding person, handling bodies, touching bloody items, or handling drug paraphernalia.

- Mouth-to-mouth resuscitation should be performed using airways with one-way valves, hand-operated bags, or other devices.

- Any exposed part of your body should be washed quickly and thoroughly after possible exposure.

- Clothing that contacts blood or other body fluids should be removed and cleaned before being worn again.

- If you have a break in your skin, cover it with an impermeable bandage before going on duty.

- Be careful when searching a drug abuser to avoid sharp or pointed objects.

- Exposed protective gear should be disposed of in a proper manner.

- Evidence items should be stored in double plastic bags and clearly labeled.

- Bodies of suspected AIDS victims should be identified with a distinctive toe tag

If you are exposed to blood or body fluids, you should document the incident. The suspected carrier should be tested for HIV antibodies. You should be tested to establish base line data, then every six weeks for a year if the carrier tests positive.

Chapter 4
REPORT WRITING

From management's point of view, writing a report is the most important part of your job. From your point of view, it's secondary. First you have to acquire the information to put in the report through investigation. You then present this information to management in a way it will be understood by someone who wasn't there, leaving no chance for the reader to misunderstand your actions or motives.

Newspaper reporters learn that stories must include who, what, where, when, why, and how. Your report is more important than a news story because it may directly affect people's lives. However, you can borrow the reporter's format.

Who must include everyone involved, whether participant or witness.

What must describe the situation as you observed it and any action taken because of your observations.

Where needs to be specific as to location, both during the event and after you acted.

When demands specific times relative to the incident itself and later actions.

Why, if known, may indicate motive for a criminal act or cause of an accident. It may also justify your actions.

How may chart the development of a situation or describe your actions in relation to the challenges presented to you.

What incidents should be reported? Company policy will decide, but, for your own protection, write up any situation in which you acted in any way. As long as there is a written record, it can be used later to show cause for actions. A report is a permanent record and must be complete, accurate, and clear.

The ABCs of report writing are Accuracy, Brevity, Clarity and Completeness. Use correct English when writing reports—not conversational English. Ambiguity is common in conversation.

It can be deadly on the job. Suppose you are sent on a call where you find two persons apparently causing a disturbance. You radio a description of the two to the dispatcher. Then one pulls a gun. "He pulled a gun," you tell the dispatcher. Who pulled a gun? When backup arrives, who does your armed colleague watch for?

A notebook is important. The basis of your report, and perhaps your testimony in court years later, is your field notebook. No one expects you to remember all the details. You may refer to your notes in court. Remember, what you bring into court is subject to subpoena. If you bring in the little spiral bound pad you carry in your shirt pocket, it (all of it) could become evidence in the case. While it's convenient, it does not constitute a field notebook.

Better that you keep your "real" notebook in a loose leaf binder and prepare your field notes with thoughtful consideration. Then, bring into court only those pages that apply to the case. If the defense counsel decides to use them as evidence, you don't lose the whole notebook.

Your field notes need to be complete, clear, and accurate. "A young scruffy-looking character in a blue outfit" tells little. How young? What made him look scruffy? What color blue, light or dark? What type of clothing? What condition was it in? Hair length, facial hair? What was the emotional condition of the witness, excited and agitated or calm and considered? Record your impressions. Record details in your notebook: date, time, location, license plates, descriptions, sequence of events, names and addresses, reminders for follow up, all facts that you will need to type in your incident report. If it's a trespass case, note the date and time you ordered the trespasser to leave. You can make your own observations of the scene. Record what you see with sufficient detail so anyone reading from your notes clearly knows what the situation was at the time. In one case an officer found a body and immediately started making notes. On the right cheek, there was a pattern of little triangular shaped cuts. They were not the cause of death. Are they significant? As it turned out, a one-armed suspect admitted to using a beverage can opener as a weapon. Suddenly, those little marks were critical evidence.

Unless you get positive identification of witnesses and other facts immediately at the scene and include them in your report, they are often lost forever. A "Catch-22" situation occurs when force must be used to subdue a subject. The more force used, the greater the stress. The greater the stress, the greater the likelihood of faulty reporting. When any amount of force is used, your report must clearly and completely state the facts justifying the type and amount of force used. Note also whether any lesser means of control were attempted and proved insufficient, such as verbal direction or unarmed physical restraint techniques. In your own self-interest, this type of report is one you do not want returned at some later date marked "incomplete."

REPORT CHECKLIST

Elements of the crime: Your local police have a field manual that identifies the elements that constitute a violation or crime. Those elements should be included in your report.

Penalty-enhancing circumstances: Some crimes carry a more severe penalty if committed while armed, or committed against a police officer or an elderly or retarded person. Those circumstances must be alleged at the time the complaint is filed.

Reasons for stop or detention: Even an obviously guilty party may go free if you don't show your reasons for initiating your action. Be specific. Court decisions have held that you must be able to state "articulable facts" to show why you did what you did, every step of the way. Draw on your experience to show why a subject's actions made you suspicious.

Basis for search and seizure: If you acted in the heat of the moment, your report must include all the facts that gave you a legal basis for acting: consent to search, contraband in plain view, imminent destruction of evidence, crime in progress. If you can cite several justifications, include them all.

Statements by suspect: Should the subject make a damaging statement, be more specific than simply saying "he admitted to the crime." Use the subject's words in a direct quote. Include everything said in explaining his actions. It might be admissible in court as a spontaneous utterance, even without advisement and waiver of rights. If it's a contrived alibi, it may do as much to convict the subject as an admission.

Statements of witnesses: If a witness appears friendly to the suspect, report the exact words. Such statements may be used to impeach the witness in court if the testimony is inconsistent. For other witnesses, some experts advise caution about reporting direct quotes. You can't testify as to what a witness told you; that's hearsay. If your report shows the victim made a statement that conflicts with the testimony, you may become a defense witness to prove prior inconsistent statements.

Suspect's demeanor: A suspect may advance a defense of diminished capacity. Carefully record your observations of the suspect's demeanor. Include in your notes observations such as "she appeared to show no signs of intoxication," or "he appeared to respond quickly and decisively to questions," or "she seemed to know where she was and the time and day," or that "he asked questions showing his awareness of the situation." Then state the questions.

Cliff hangers: For instance, your report shows a crime was committed in January and a report submitted to police in July. If the report doesn't explain why there was a six-month delay, a defense attorney will file a motion for dismissal for lack of a speedy trial. And the prosecutor won't have the necessary information to respond.

Reports and statements of witnesses and perpetrators should be written on company forms or on plain paper, never on forms supplied by the police. Remember, you have wider latitude than the police. You needn't "Mirandize" the person. You have a right to search on your employer's property, the police don't. However, if there's any indication you were acting as an agent of the police, all the rules that apply to the police will then apply to you. For instance, you can obtain a confession in writing and it will stand up in court. But put the same written confession on a police department form and the defense will argue in court that you were acting as an agent of the police, hence the confession is inadmissible because no Miranda warning was given.

Your report serves many purposes. It may be the basis for follow-up investigation by the police. It may be the basis for a formal complaint. It may be used by the police crime analysis section to develop new crime prevention procedures. It will surely be subpoenaed by the defense attorney in the discovery process when the case goes to court.

Chapter 5
LAW

The United States Constitution affords citizens protections against unwarranted actions by government or its agents, police. The security officer is not a "government agent," and can do things that police cannot do. However, the fine lines of distinction are dimming. Citizens don't care whether a badge reads "Security" or "Police." They are going to claim their constitutional rights. You must be aware of the challenges police face for the times when your cases will be turned over to police.

English common law was the foundation on which American law was built. Now it is more complicated. To the United States Constitution add the constitutions of each state, along with federal and state statutes, published court decisions, town ordinances, and regulations by regulatory agencies.

STATUTORY LAW

Statutory law is simply the body of law including statutes enacted by the legislature. The common term statutory rape refers to sexual intercourse with an underage person. Even if the person consents, it is considered rape because the statute defines it as such.

COMMON LAW

Common law, case law, and judicial precedent are the collected body of published court decisions that have the effect of law. However, since courts cover geographical areas, their decisions affect only those areas. Attorneys may use case decisions of other courts to bolster their arguments, but it's only an argument and not the "law" in your area. Therefore, while common law is used as an all-inclusive term, its meaning can vary from one jurisdiction to another.

This isn't so complex once you remember the details of the United States Constitution. No state law may contravene the basic law of the land.

UNITED STATES CONSTITUTION

The United States Constitution went into effect in 1789 and set up our form of government. It divides the federal government into three parts: legislative (Article I), executive (Article II), and judicial (Article III), and one branch may not encroach upon the province of another. The legislature writes laws. The executive branch enforces laws. The judiciary interprets laws. The Constitution defines the functions that are appropriately performed by the federal government—for example, maintaining a defense force, handling mail, making treaties, coining money, declaring war—and it limits the powers of states in these areas.

THE BILL OF RIGHTS

The first ten amendments were ratified in 1791 as the Bill of Rights. They address concerns not specifically covered in the basic document. Since the original document was written, other amendments have been added over the years.

AMENDMENT PURPOSE
First
> Guarantees freedom of speech, religion, press, peaceable assembly, and redress of grievances.

Second
> Prohibits infringement of the right of the people to keep and bear arms.

Third
> Prohibits quartering soldiers in a home without the consent of the owner.

Fourth

Prohibits unreasonable search and seizure. Requires "probable cause" supported by oath, and particular description of places to be searched and persons or things to be seized.

Fifth

Requires indictment by a grand jury in major crimes. Prohibits putting a person in double jeopardy, confiscation of property without just compensation, deprivation of life, liberty, or property without due process of law, or compelling persons to incriminate themselves.

Sixth

Guarantees the right to a speedy trial and counsel. (The 1963 case of *Gideon v. Wainwright* defined the right to counsel: if there is a likelihood of imposing a jail sentence, a defendant must have counsel, even if he or she is indigent.)

Seventh

Guarantees trial by jury.

Eighth

Prohibits excessive bail and cruel or unusual punishment.

Ninth

States that listing rights in the Constitution shall not be construed to deny or disparage other rights retained by the people.

Tenth

Provides that powers not delegated to the federal government, or prohibited to the states, are reserved to the states or to the people.

OTHER AMENDMENTS

Another amendment important to the security officer was added in 1868. The Fourteenth Amendment guarantees due process of law. It states, "Nor shall any State deprive any person of life, liberty, or property, without due process of law; nor deny to any person within its jurisdiction equal protection of the laws."

Also, the Fourth Amendment is of particular importance to the security officer. "The right of the people to be secure in their persons, houses, papers, and effects, against unreasonable searches and seizures, shall not be violated, and no warrants shall issue, but upon probable cause, supported by oath or affirmation, and particularly describing the place to be searched, and the person or things to be seized."

Probable cause is a concept that applies only to police. In the security field, it is called reasonable grounds to believe. But a key word in the Fourth Amendment is "unreasonable." When police apply for a warrant, they must include as much information as possible to show that the conclusion is reasonable. If you develop a case to turn over to police, they need all the information you have to show sufficient "reasonable grounds to believe" in order to give them "probable cause."

REASONABLE GROUNDS TO BELIEVE

The legal principle for a police officer's actions is probable cause. Briefly, probable cause is defined as the facts and circumstances sufficient to lead a reasonable person to believe that a crime has been or is being committed, and that the suspect has committed or is committing it, *Beck v. Ohio (1964)*. Remember, probable cause does not apply to the security officer, but courts have applied the principle in terms of "reasonable grounds to believe" where a security officer was involved.

In deciding whether reasonable grounds exist, you may consider information known at the time and the facts leading to your action. To help establish reasonable grounds, the security officer can rely on hearsay, admissions, statements of fellow officers, witnesses, and observations. For example, you see a person acting in such a way that you become suspicious. The officer you relieved said that a person matching this suspect's description had been observed. Next, you see the suspect running down the street. Those actions in themselves aren't enough to convince you that a crime is involved. But, shortly thereafter, a victim informs you that a crime has been committed. The suspect's actions, along with the victim's information, may establish reasonable grounds.

The Fourth Amendment permits police to augment their senses with tools provided by science and technology. For example, *United States v. Knotts (1983)* concluded that no search existed when an electronic homing device was used to track a purchased container to the defendant's cabin. *California v. Ciraolo (1986)* upheld warrantless surveillance flights by aircraft over a drug dealer's property.

Other Supreme Court decisions have established precedents:

Plain view. If police inadvertently see incriminating evidence in plain view, in a place they have a right to be for a proper reason, they can seize it, *Coolidge v. New Hampshire (1971)*.

Exigent circumstances. Because police officers are sworn to protect the public, they are expected to act immediately in emergency situations—for instance, when drugs are being flushed down a toilet, or screams are emitting from inside a closed room indicating someone is in grave danger. In emergency situations, police don't have time to obtain a warrant or ask permission to enter a dwelling, *Mincey v. Arizona (1978)*.

This principle holds true for the security officer within the employer's premises.

As soon as possible, write a report that clearly explains all the reasons that led you to believe immediate action was necessary. Whenever you act without a supervisor's overview, an attorney for the plaintiff in a civil suit will look for a way to discredit your action. The United States Supreme Court has held that a warrantless search of a home is unconstitutional without exigent circumstances, *Payton v. New York (1980)*. To arrest a subject in the home of a third party requires both an arrest and a search warrant, *Steagold v. United States (1981)*.

You may make a reasonable search of areas within the suspect's reach or distance. Necessity demands that you protect yourself. Through a search you can make sure the person has no weapons, access to items that would aid escape, or evidence that could be destroyed. Any search beyond these limits of time and area requires a warrant.

INTERPRETING THE LAW

All laws are interpreted by the courts. While you may read a law one way, how a court of your jurisdiction reads it will prevail.

Article IV, Section 2 of the United States Constitution states, "The Citizens of each State shall be entitled to all Privileges and Immunities of Citizens in the several States." Amendment XIV,

Section 1, says, "No State shall make or enforce any law which shall abridge the privileges or immunities of the citizens of the United States."

This means that you don't need an operator's license for every state you drive through. And that a bride and groom, for example, were legally married when they visited a honeymoon resort in a neighboring state. However, my state granted me a permit to carry a concealed pistol or revolver. Other states do not recognize this permit, and courts have upheld this as "reasonable" restriction.

The security officer is not expected to be an attorney. Even attorneys specialize because they can't know everything. But you must understand the law as it applies to you. For example, under the principle of "fruit of the poisoned tree," if you violate a suspect's rights, any evidence gathered as a result is inadmissible. This can destroy the whole case. The next section explains this principle in more detail.

A security officer on duty is ready to protect employees and assets at a moment's notice. You are expected to act, at times, on your own initiative. When you act, you must have reasonable grounds. The action must be "fresh"—that is, it must relate to an event that is occurring now or occurred only a short while ago. A "short while ago" usually is measured in minutes rather than hours.

FRUIT OF THE POISONED TREE

"Fruit of the poisoned tree" is the principle that legal evidence gathered illegally is not admissible as evidence.

In one case, *Taylor v. Alabama (1982)*, a grocery store was robbed. A person, already in custody on unrelated charges, told a policeman he heard that Omar Taylor was involved. The officer arrested Taylor without a warrant, acting solely on that information. The defendant was advised of his rights and taken to the stationhouse. There, he was fingerprinted and again advised of his rights. In a lineup, victims failed to identify Taylor, but police found his fingerprints on items taken from the grocery. After a brief visit with his girlfriend and a neighbor, and some six hours after his arrest, the defendant signed a waiver of his rights and gave a written confession.

At trial, Taylor's defense counsel objected that the evidence of his waiver and confession were the fruits of his illegal arrest. The judge overruled and Taylor was convicted. On appeal, the United States Supreme Court voted five to four to overturn the conviction. They found a lack of probable cause for the original arrest. No matter how many times his rights were read later, anything that followed the illegal arrest is fruit of the poisoned tree.

This exclusionary rule has been eased somewhat in recent years. Once, the slightest technical discrepancy was enough to invalidate a warrant. Now, if an officer acts on information believed to be true, but it turns out it's not, the United States Supreme Court states in *United States v. Leon, 468 United States 897 (1984)* that the officer acted in good faith.

Such nuances affect the security officer's daily life, and they can change from day to day. The information presented here is accurate at the time of writing, but it's not gospel. The final authority is your company's legal counsel. And his or her advice is valid only at the time you ask the question. The law can change.

Cases cited in this book were decided by the United States Supreme Court. Their decisions apply all over the country. State courts have published decisions that apply in that state. Those that affect your function as a security officer should be cited in your training.

Chapter 6
DETENTION

The Fourth Amendment of the U.S. Constitution addresses the right of police to detain a suspect. While it does not apply to non-sworn security officers, it does apply to security officers holding special police commissions. You must be aware of the concerns that will arise when your actions lead to a police arrest.

An arrest is a restraint, a denial of freedom of movement. It happens when persons believe they are in an officer's custody—not free to leave. Once denied freedom of movement, a person is arrested, *California v. Beheler (1983)*. In virtually every state, security officers do not have the power of arrest.

But a security officer can detain a person while investigating a situation. A detention is the holding of a person pending confinement or release. You have the right to maintain the status quo while you are checking a situation. A witness may be held to determine identity, for example. It must be temporary and last only as long as it takes to confirm or refute your suspicions. This non-criminal detention is permitted under the Fourth Amendment.

Some states have laws defining citizen's arrest. You are a citizen, but the law varies so widely it's not possible to generalize. Where such laws exist, they must be understood thoroughly. A citizen's arrest can lead to complicated legal problems. Law enforcement officers from across the country strongly advise security officers to shy away from making a citizen's arrest.

A poorly handled arrest may be held illegal and can lead to civil liability suits. For instance, the security officer in a retail store may detain a shoplifter for police. Even if your state law says you may make an arrest when you've witnessed the commission of a felony, detain the offender. You cannot arrest on a warrant, and there may not be a "resisting arrest" law pertaining to private citizens. Thus, you cannot arrest for resisting. However, if the subject assaults you after being detained, that constitutes another offense which you can add to your report to the police. Let the responding police officer be the arresting officer.

FIRST ENCOUNTER

When you first face a suspect, a mistake on your part could make any evidence you develop unusable in court, should your investigation lead to a complaint to police. Remember the fruit of the poisoned tree. Your conduct is governed by rules that depend on your knowledge of the suspect and the crime at the time you confront the suspect.

You have reason to believe an adult male, for example, has knowledge of a crime, but no reason to think he's involved. You can question him without concern over self-incrimination or right to counsel. Even if you suspect he's involved, you may still question him, but it must be clear that he is not obligated to answer and is free to stop answering and leave at any time. If you make him think he is not free to go, then the rules of conduct based on the Fifth Amendment apply, and that's a matter for the police.

Once you restrain a person, search and seizure rules take effect. Ordinarily, a person is not detained if you just ask for identification. But if you take additional steps, it's a detention.

If you have knowledge of facts that lead you to believe someone is involved in criminal activity, you may stop and briefly detain the person for questioning. But you must be able to point out specific facts to support your suspicion, that it is not just a hunch. Your decision to act may be based on your evaluation of facts, including reasonable conclusions that your experience enables you to draw from those facts. If you cannot explain all this to a judge's satisfaction, any evidence you discover could be useless in prosecuting the person.

During a stop, you may question the suspect, have the suspect viewed by a witness, and detain the suspect while you pursue other avenues of investigation. The Supreme Court has held that this may even include fingerprinting. But time is critical. A detention without reasonable grounds must be brief, minutes not hours. You may not detain a person any longer than reasonably necessary to accomplish the legitimate purpose of the stop.

Your right to move a suspect from where the stop occurred is uncertain. Some courts have held the suspect may be taken a short distance to be viewed by a witness, but others have disagreed. Calling police to take the suspect to the police station would likely make your detention an arrest, for which police must have probable cause. If you discover nothing during the stop to give the police probable cause to arrest, you must allow the suspect to leave.

STOP AND FRISK

Even though you lack sufficient information to establish reasonable grounds, you don't have to ignore suspicious activity. In the case of *Terry v. Ohio (1968),* the Supreme Court recognized that an officer may have to briefly detain a person to establish identity, to maintain the status quo, or to conduct further investigation. If you reasonably believe the suspect may be armed, you can do a protective stop and frisk, a "patdown," to ensure your own safety, but not to discover evidence. The Supreme Court has held that this rule applies to security officers.

If you should happen to find evidence during this limited search, it would be admissible later because your actions to that point were proper. However, in some states it may extend only to weapons or your employer's stolen property. Narcotics and other contraband should be left for discovery by the responding police officer.

It's up to you to explain your reasons for doing a stop and frisk. If you can't satisfy a judge that it was proper, any evidence you found could be thrown out.

MIRANDA WARNING

Only on television do cops ask, "Did you read him his rights?" Cops don't presume, they read them again. The Miranda rule does not apply to security officers, unless you are acting as an instrument of the government or have special police powers. If a police officer asks you to stake out a location and it leads to an apprehension, you are acting as an agent of the police and all the rules apply. If you're acting on your own or for your security service, you are a citizen. You do not "read him his rights."

You may like a technique that Asset Protection Officer Jeff Gershaneck uses, "I make it a habit in all petty theft cases to have the subject write a brief explanation why they committed the theft. You should see the defense attorney's face when they are presented with what amounts to a full written confession!"

Chapter 7
SEARCH AND SEIZURE

$\mathbf{A}$ search or seizure of evidence off the employer's premises should always be done by police. The security officer should search only within the employer's premises, where they have special privileges. The Founding Fathers thought it important to include in the Bill of Rights the Fourth Amendment with its guarantee against unreasonable searches and seizures by government. A court might extend the same principles to unreasonable searches and seizures by you as the agent of your employer.

Even within the employer's premises, if the employee has an expectation of privacy the situation can be delicate. For instance, if the company provides a locker and a lock for which it retains a key with the employee's consent, then you have the right to search. If the employee provides the lock and key, the interior of the locker could be considered private property by the court. If there are reasonable grounds to believe the locker contains contraband, contact the police and let them decide whether to apply for a warrant. Case law has established that the contents of a desk will be viewed as the employee's private property, if the desk was assigned to that employee alone. If it's a communal desk, it's fair game.

This protection extends to persons, houses, papers, property, or anything in which a person has manifested a reasonable expectation of privacy, *United States v. Katz (1967)*. Protection extends not only to the building, but also to its "curtilage"—the open areas immediately adjacent to a dwelling, i.e. the lawn, or more specifically "area around the home to which the activity of home life extends." It does not offer protection where one cannot reasonably expect privacy, such as open fields or public places.

While the security officer is more at liberty than police to search on the premises, remember that the searches are to protect yourself (looking for weapons) and to protect company assets (looking for stolen property). The limitations of the Fourth Amendment do not apply as you are not an agent of the state. If drugs, burglar tools, or other contraband are found incidental to a search for weapons or stolen property, they are admissible evidence. However, if your search was primarily to find such contraband, a court might hold it unreasonable.

Ask the subject's permission to search. Try to get the consent in writing. If consent is refused, consider if there is reasonable grounds to hold the subject for the police.

PLAIN VIEW DOCTRINE

If the security officer has the right to be present in a place, any evidence or contraband in plain view can be seized and is admissible in court. For example, you stop a car at the factory gate, look in at the driver's identification and see a package on the front seat. Experience tells you it is illegal narcotics. You can seize it and detain the operator for police. The key here is that you have a right to be where you are. If a person invited you into his home and you spotted drugs, you can act. Remember, the Fourth Amendment does not apply to citizens. Of course, the prudent course would be to note as many details as possible and turn them over to police.

If you have the right to be in a place and you see contraband in plain view, you can seize it. But if you are trespassing, whatever evidence you seize may be excluded, *Coolidge v. New Hampshire (1971)*.

OPEN FIELDS DOCTRINE

In one case, two narcotics officers went to a farm to check reports of marijuana being grown. They stopped their car at the locked gate and followed a foot path around the gate and down a road passing a barn and parked camper. They found a field of marijuana more than a mile from the defendant's house. They arrested him. The defendant moved to suppress the evidence, claiming violation of the Fourth Amendment. The Supreme Court held the entry and search to be lawful because protection extends to "persons, houses, papers, and effects," but not open fields. This term may include any unoccupied or undeveloped area outside the curtilage. A thickly wooded area could be an open field under this definition, *Oliver v. United States (1984)*.

CONSENT SEARCHES

The security officer has an advantage over the police officer. You're not an agent of the government and you're on private property. With due notice, you have the right to search whatever you please. If a sign is posted, "All packages subject to search," it is a company rule. You can deny entry onto the premises if a person refuses to have a package searched.

Where there is company housing on company property over which you have jurisdiction, the rules of search that apply to police are likely to be applied to you. You should understand these rules.

A person consenting to a search must have authority to do so, i.e. have a right to possess the premises, be an adult, be the owner of the house, or occupant of the hotel room. An adult may consent to the search of a child's room but not the other way around. A parent may not consent to the search of an adult child's room, if it is used exclusively by the adult child. A minor child's consent isn't likely to stand up, but an adult child can consent to the search of jointly used areas. A person responsible for caring for the property may consent to a search.

A tenant is the responsible consenter for a warrantless search. Entry into a rented premises at the request of the landlord was held unreasonable, even though the tenant was schedule to vacate the premises that same day.

Anyone may waive a right or privilege to which he or she is entitled. But courts look at such waivers carefully. After all, these protections evolved because of historical abuse. You have to show that the person made some positive action to waive a right of privacy. You may have a printed form to be signed but a verbal consent is permitted when you can corroborate it, *Schneckloth v. Bustamonte (1973)*.

The search cannot extend beyond the terms of the consent in either time or area. If the resident agrees to the search of a

The security officer is not an agent of the government. With due notice, you have the right to search packages.

hotel room, you may not search the rest of the suite. The resident can stop the search at any time by simply revoking consent.

55

MOVABLE VEHICLES

If police stop a motorist, and it develops that there is probable cause to believe contraband is in the vehicle, the contraband could be lost if police took time to get a warrant. Thus, they are permitted to search even the locked compartments, *Carroll v. United States (1925), United States v. Ross (1982), New York v. Belton (1981).* However, the right to search depends on probable cause. In your case, reasonable grounds. If you have reason to believe the vehicle contains a stolen stereo, for example, you can't look for it in the glove compartment.

Such warrantless searches require the same essential elements of probable cause that police need for a warrant. And you must be able to show those elements were known prior to the search. If you detained a motorist because you had reason to believe the vehicle contained contraband, you must be able to explain all these reasons to police when you turn the case over to them.

LUGGAGE

Luggage is a common repository of personal effects and people have a greater expectation of privacy in their luggage. If you suspect a drug courier of transporting contraband in luggage, for example, it may be better to detain the luggage for police and let them get a warrant before it's opened, *Arkansas v. Sanders (1979).*

Chapter 8
CRIMES

The security officer's actions are influenced, governed, and regulated by law, as well as by company policies. You must understand the law. What constitutes a crime, felony, misdemeanor, or infraction is determined by the laws of a particular state or jurisdiction. If you take some enforcement action and detain an offender for police, you could very well commit a crime yourself.

Most crimes are classified either as felonies, punishable by more than a year in prison, or misdemeanors, punishable by up to a year in jail. That also defines the difference between a jail and a prison. A jail houses prisoners for up to one year, a prison holds inmates sentenced for more than a year.

For a misdemeanor or felony conviction, it must be proved that the person acted with wrongful intent—negligently, recklessly, knowingly, or purposely. These are offenses that you would normally turn over to police.

Then there are infractions, violations or petty offenses. In the police view, these are punishable by a fine with no time behind bars. In your view, they are punishable by company disciplinary action. Infractions include parking improperly or running a stop sign. No criminal intent is required for a person to be guilty of an infraction. These offenses would normally be handled within the company.

MALA PER SE

Acts that are bad in and of themselves—mala per se—include such crimes as murder, arson, robbery, larceny, burglary, assault, rape, and kidnapping. These are crimes everywhere, but there are degrees and localized definitions of each. For instance, robbery implies that physical force was used against a victim. While burglary implies that property was stolen from an empty building.

If, while committing a larceny, the perpetrator uses or threatens physical force to compel the owner to give up property, then it's robbery. It can be robbery in different degrees, depending on whether the actor causes injury, is armed, threatens or represents possession of deadly weapon or instrument, or is aided by another person.

Larceny means wrongfully and intentionally depriving someone of property. This could include embezzlement, false pretense or promise, extortion, receiving stolen property, theft of services, shoplifting, fraud, or failing to return rented property. Degrees in larceny are determined by the value of the property taken.

MALA PROHIBITA

Crimes that are bad only because society decided by an act of legislation that they are crimes are called mala prohibita. Such laws are generally founded in common sense. A liquor dealer is in the business of selling alcoholic beverages, which is not a crime. But if they are sold to a minor, the dealer can lose a license to do business.

ADMINISTRATIVE REGULATION

Society elects officials who establish boards and commissions to administer a particular activity, and legislatures sometimes delegate to these persons or agencies the power to publish regulations that have the force of law.

An example might be the illegal dumping of hazardous wastes. While on patrol, you see a truck rolling drums into a gully at night in a remote area. Your suspicions are aroused, so you investigate. You find the drums contain a substance included in hazardous waste regulations. That is a crime.

ELEMENTS AND DEGREE OF AN OFFENSE

Elements define a particular offense. For example, to commit murder in most jurisdictions, a person must intend to cause the death of a person and actually cause it either directly or by suicide through force, duress, or deception. Presenting crimes in terms of elements defines what you must prove.

An offense may be further classified according to degree. The seriousness of the offense is graded according to specific elements of the offense. To continue the wrongful death example, murder in the first degree requires both willful and premeditated intent to kill and the act caused the death. What if the actor only intended to seriously injure, but caused the death? That may be manslaughter in the first degree. If the actor's recklessness causes death, it could be manslaughter in the second degree.

Assault is a broad term that includes crimes ranging from a felony to a misdemeanor. If the actor intends to cause serious injury, actually causes serious injury, and uses a deadly weapon or dangerous instrument, in most states it's first degree assault. Take away the weapon and it's assault two. If the intent was only to injure, rather than seriously injure, and the actor causes injury, it's assault three. If the actor recklessly risks serious injury with indifference to human life, it may be reckless endangerment one. Take away the indifference and it's reckless endangerment two.

When you're involved in the detection of a crime and detention of a criminal, it's time to call the police. But since it was your case until you determined that a crime had been committed and your suspect most likely committed it, you become the prime witness. You must define the offense for the responding police officer and probably explain your actions in court.

You need to study the statutes in your state regarding a citizen's use of force, and what constitutes the crimes of trespass, larceny, burglary, and others. Also study the following torts that you may be accused of: assault, battery, false imprisonment, defamation, neglectful infliction of emotional distress, intentional infliction of emotional distress, and invasion of privacy.

59

Chapter 9
INTERVIEWS AND INTERROGATION

The security officer must determine the facts of a situation to decide if there is reason to refer a case to police. An important part of making this determination is interview and interrogation. An interview is a talk with a friendly and cooperative witness or victim, someone willing to help, who has no apparent reason to lie. However, a person who is friendly with the accused could be biased and protective of the suspect. The interview is an effort to develop accurate information from a reasonably cooperative person.

An interrogation is a talk with an unfriendly and uncooperative person—the accused or a co-conspirator. This person normally has something to conceal. An appearance of cooperation may be a ploy to mask deception.

Sometimes the distinction is not clear. For instance, the supply person who just lost valuable materials from the stockroom could be the "inside man."

INTERVIEW

Your company may prefer that you leave interviewing to your supervisor or a trained investigator. But you need to talk with people to determine if you should call the investigator. Whenever you talk with anyone, you need to establish that you are in control of the conversation. How much control obviously depends on the situation. Know what kinds of information you need to discover and what questions to ask.

If an Hispanic subject can't speak English and you can't speak Spanish, you have a problem. Find out beforehand if you are going to need an interpreter.

There are two schools of thought regarding the interviewer's

The interview is an effort to develop accurate information from a reasonably cooperative person.

dress and demeanor. One holds that the security officer should be well dressed and look professional, in uniform or a business suit. The other theory is that skill is more important than appearance, especially if your normal duty dress is informal and you don't want to intimidate the witness with a uniform.

There are also two schools of thought on the best location for the interview. At a scene, you don't have much choice as you interview witnesses. Getting the information while it's fresh is more important than moving to pleasant surroundings.

When setting up an interview, the choice of location depends on the interviewer—where you can function best and where the interviewee will be most inclined to give you information. A relaxed and friendly atmosphere seems to work best. You may prefer to meet a witness somewhere other than at security headquarters, at a home or office, if possible, or other familiar place. On the other hand, a particular witness may more freely discuss the subject under slightly intimidating circumstances.

Some witnesses feel secure in the environment of your interview room.

When you're trying to develop a sequence of events, begin the interview with the witness who was most directly involved. This may be the victim or a bystander. They probably had the longest look at the suspect, so can give the most accurate description of the subject and the sequence of events. This gives you the broadest picture possible, and may suggest other questions.

Someone standing outside an office when a theft occurred could have information not available to those inside. For instance, the suspect ran out and jumped into a car. (Of course, if you find this witness first as you arrive, your primary duty would be to get the vehicle description so you can relay it to police.)

INTERVIEW POSITION OR STANCE

Consider the possibility that a subject being interviewed could become hostile. For instance, suppose the subject you are interviewing lunged at you suddenly? Stand in a position that translates into immediate defense and counterattack. Stand more than an arm's length away, turned a quarter way toward your strong side. Keep your hands up in front of you, perhaps holding a notebook. This is a boxer's stance, although it doesn't look like it. From this position you can immediately fend off a blow with your weak arm as your strong arm counter punches or reaches for your baton. You are prepared for anything.

TAKING STATEMENTS

It's better to let witnesses tell their stories in their own way, preferably without interruption. This narration brings out the main points as the witness sees them. Fill in the details later, if necessary, with further questions.

When taking statements from more than one witness, talk with each individually, separate and apart from others. Eyewitness testimony is questionable at best. People don't remember every detail. One person will remember different details than another. Witnesses unsure of themselves will be influenced by what others say. Keep witnesses apart prior to the interview so they don't have a chance to concoct a story.

Bias on the part of a witness is not lying. It's human nature to shade the truth or slant the facts to support one's own beliefs. Experienced interviewers call it "selective memory."

Handling inadequate responses challenges an interviewer's skill. A strained facial expression could imply that the person is holding back some information. Witnesses may be purposefully evasive, or just may not remember. By posing the right questions, you can often prod their memory or catch them off guard.

The principles of getting information from someone are:

1. **Be objective**—the witness has something you need and want.
2. **Keep yourself out of the incident**—don't get personally involved.
3. **Be positive**—pay attention, be responsive and supportive.
4. **Listen carefully to answers**. You ask, "When did you come to work here?" The subject answers, "I came from Des Moines." It's surprising how many officers won't hear that the question was not answered.
5. **Never suggest answers**—your question must be generic.
6. **Avoid conflict**—never argue.
7. **Verify statements**—measure information you get against what you already know.
8. **Be adaptable**—sense the mood of the interviewee and make the conversation flow.
9. **Be reasonable and understanding**—in other words, be easy to talk to.
10. **Never embarrass the subject**.

The purpose of the interview is to seek information for your report. If you take written statements, witnesses are less likely to change their story. It becomes part of the permanent record. Then have the witness sign it. If the witness refuses, write "refused to sign" in the signature spot and ask the witness to initial your entry, not sign it. If you correct the typed copy, have each correction initialed by the person giving the statement.

ASK THE RIGHT QUESTIONS

Most field interviews are conducted to enable you to fill out a report, so ask questions that will provide the information called for in the report. Filling out an accident report is usually done right in the car, perhaps with the subject in the back seat so you can ask questions right off the report form.

While narrating a story, a subject may need encouragement. Nodding your head at appropriate times, looking the subject in the eye, and assuming a supportive posture imparts the feeling that you are interested in what is being said and encourages the subject to continue.

Avoid asking "leading" questions during an interview. The subject may need prompting, however, which is different from leading. A leading question introduces an element that hasn't been brought up before. Even if the complaint is aggravated assault, never ask, "Did you see the weapon?" before the witness says a weapon was involved. Instead, prompt, "Did you see the suspect holding anything in his hands?" The subject must tell you there was a weapon present.

Some other examples of prompting questions: "What did you do then?" "Why did you do that?" "What else did you see at that moment?" "Did you hear anything else right then?" "Was someone else there at the time?" Note that these questions carry no implications.

Develop your own prompting questions to ensure that you learn all that is pertinent in a case. Also learn to note in the report if the victim is elderly, infirm, or retarded to justify a more serious charge.

You need not apologize for taking notes. You need specific information to fill out a report, and no one expects you to remember all of the details. A person who is frightened in the presence of officers may experience heightened anxiety at the sight of a notebook. To put the person at ease, ask "Do you mind if I make a list of the items that were taken?" Or a comment, "Let me make a note of that so I'll be sure to remember the details."

This is the "velvet glove" approach to interviewing. You need a light touch when dealing with co-workers, especially when they are trying to be helpful. If you run into a memory block, real or feigned, divert attention to another point, then work back to the blocked information from a different direction. Such a shift may give the witness a different memory trigger, or catch intentionally evasive subjects off guard.

Be tactful in dealing with a witness. Don't use pressure over discrepancies in a statement, nor call a comment a "lie," even if you know it is. Instead, refer to "points" in a story, minor matters that need to be "clarified." It could be that the witness just doesn't want to admit lack of knowledge, or doesn't remember.

A good interviewer reads body language. The witness who is hiding something may lean back with arms folded against the chest. One whose arms are open and leans forward attentively maybe more eager to help or may be promoting a tall tale. Remember, too, that the interviewer can also telegraph thoughts and reactions by gestures and expressions that can be picked up by the interviewee.

INTERROGATION

The security officer shouldn't need to conduct an interrogation. By that time the case is turned over to police who are trained in this game of wits. Actually, questioning is an interplay between two people. You need to develop a rapport with the suspect and encourage further talking.

Downplaying the moral seriousness of the offense, particularly in sex cases, may encourage the suspect to talk. Or, you might play one accomplice against another. Sympathy may also help to open up a suspect.

Remember that a principal psychological factor in a successful interrogation is privacy. When someone confides in another, it is done out of earshot of others. However, you may want a witness present, especially if the interviewee is of the opposite sex.

Be tactful in your choice of words. Avoid "steal" and "confess." Better are "take," and "tell the truth." Don't say, "You're lying to me." Say, "You haven't told me the whole truth." Your language should be in an idiom understood by the suspect.

Treating the subject with decency and respect can be rewarding. To avoid any taint of coercion, don't use restraints in the interview room. The interviewer should not be armed. A guard can always be posted just outside the door.

Because a citizen is not required to issue a Miranda warning, you could even take a confession from the suspect and it can be used in court. However, you must guard against using duress, or a threat of dire consequences if the subject does not cooperate. Never threaten to tell a spouse or employer. Defense counsel will call it coercion, even extortion. Obviously, obtain any such statement of guilt before police arrive. Once they arrive, Miranda and all the other rules apply.

"SIZING UP" SUSPECTS

Evaluating a suspect to determine the techniques and tactics appropriate to each situation is a skill developed through experience. You might confront a suspect whose guilt is reasonably certain with that belief, hoping to prompt a confession or incriminating statement. If the suspect's guilt is uncertain, then you have to feel your way around.

Suspects who commit crimes against individuals are usually emotional. They may have a troubled conscience. The sympathetic approach is likely to be successful. Those who commit crimes for financial gain are more likely to be unemotional. A factual analysis is better, using techniques that appeal to common sense and reasoning.

Chapter 10
PHYSICAL FITNESS

A former police chief became so concerned that the unique physical demands of law enforcement weren't being met that he quit his job and went into full-time fitness training. I asked him, "Just how much time would an officer have to invest to maintain a high-performance conditioning level?"

"Once we've identified just what it is a particular situation needs, a fitness program could require as little as one hour, three days a week."

That isn't much to ask of a person whose job performance depends on good physical conditioning.

EXERCISE TARGETS

Your exercise program should address four targets:

1. **Cardiovascular and respiratory fitness.** Sudden cardiac arrest is a major threat to police officers. A properly designed program improves heart function, improves blood circulation, and increases lung capacity. By training through aerobic conditioning, you'll find yourself better able to exert the explosive power sometimes needed to handle a situation.
2. **Muscle strength and stamina.** Your punch power isn't increased by doing biceps curls; it's exercised by punching, by doing the function you want to improve. A qualified law enforcement physical training instructor can devise many simple routines that address the strengths a security officer needs.
3. **Joint flexibility.** If you have freedom of movement, you can better perform defensive techniques. If stiff muscles and joints cause performance to suffer, lower back problems may

follow. Lower back pain and back injuries are major problems for security officers.

4. **Low body fat.** Excess body fat impairs coordinated body movement. Fat literally gets in the way.

MENTAL WELL-BEING

Mental preparedness is too often ignored in security training. Yet, its importance is obvious in the concise definition given by the editorial director of Law and Order magazine, Bruce Cameron.

"Mental preparedness is simply having made up your mind that you will do whatever an officer needs to do when called upon—whether shooting someone who is threatening a life, wrestling a giant drunk to the floor, or jumping into an icy river to save someone. Not many officers are properly conditioned during training on how to think positively about their duties. They get good instruction on how to perform their duties, but little in regard to mental preparation."

Mental attitudes are critical for survival. They must become instinctive. All the physical skills in the world are fruitless if you aren't mentally prepared. There are a host of elements that ensure your success in a confrontation beyond the simple attributes of ability, power, speed, strength, balance, and reaction time. Alertness, the awareness of where you are in relation to all things in your environment, is the overriding mental element. If you're not ready when it's time to act, your physical skills won't help.

Jeff Cooper, a nationally known combat shooting instructor, developed a color code scheme to measure awareness levels that police trainers have enthusiastically adopted:

White—You are home watching television, unaware of your surroundings.

Yellow—Now you are aware of your surroundings, relaxed but alert. You are mentally prepared.

Orange—You are aware of something specific in your surroundings that has caught your attention. Perhaps it will become a threat. You analyze the risks to yourself and others, and consider potential reactions.

To survive, the security officer must practice the skills learned in class. *(Dave Thorstenson)*

Red—You are ready to do what needs to be done. You may decide to move in or back off, depending on the circumstances. You have decided on a plan, so your reaction will be quick and sure.

Black—You have no choice. An assault has started. If you aren't mentally prepared, you panic.

You must go from white (unaware) to black (shot at) in a fraction of a second. If you haven't followed the crucial self-training—constant anticipation of an attack—you may well be added to the dead officer statistics.

With anticipation comes preparedness. Under normal circumstances, a security officer on duty should always be in at least condition yellow.

Once you commit to react to a threat, be decisive. A mind cluttered with liability issues, company policies, and other diversions will cause hesitation. That hesitation can be fatal. Make up your mind about those "what ifs" beforehand, so when you need to act, you can.

Before you can legally use force on another person, the force must be justified under the circumstances, and it must be no more than is reasonable and necessary.

Physical aggression can't be used except to defend yourself or a third person against what you reasonably believe to be an imminent threat. You can choose the means of attack and the technique, and you need not telegraph this in advance. Gaining the element of surprise makes a technique more effective.

Once you have decided that you have the right and obligation to use force, use it like you mean it. Be aggressive. If you decide to apply a pain compliance technique, use enough force to make it work. If you draw your baton, use it—hard and properly. End the confrontation with whatever force is necessary, as quickly as you can. This reduces the risks to all involved.

Aggressiveness must be learned. It's not human nature. Learning to be assertive is part of defensive training.

To execute any defensive technique, act quickly to exploit the advantage of surprise. Speed is essential, including speed of thought. Don't stop to ask yourself if the aggressor really meant to swing that lead pipe at you. Quick thinking is as important as quick hands or feet.

Remaining cool and calm in a confrontation is a prerequisite to successfully ending it. Learn to control your emotions, and you can control the situation.

MENTAL DEFENSE TRAINING

Training is a small price to pay to develop the skills and habits that enable you to win and survive. The adage that you will perform under stress what you have been trained to perform is not quite correct. You will probably perform much worse in a serious confrontation than you ever did in training. So, to survive, you need to exercise continually the skills you learned in class. And you can do it in your head.

Suppose an attacker leaped out from a dark corner holding a gun. What would you do? Draw and shoot? Or dive for cover? And where is cover?

If you can visualize going through the motions of a newly learned technique, it will improve your ability to respond quickly. While there is no substitute for good, hard, comprehensive physical practice, you still need the mental conditioning to enhance your response and remain alert in more mundane circumstances.

The one emotion that can't be contrived is the one that makes the greatest difference in a real threat: fear. Unlike fights on television, real confrontations aren't logical, patterned, give-and-take brawls. They are a flurry of hitting and screaming, kicking and shoving. You must mentally train for the attack that is certain to be sudden, vicious, and perhaps overwhelming.

Chapter 11
ALTERNATIVES TO PHYSICAL CONFLICT

The last thing a security officer wants is to be involved in physical conflict. But violence is on the increase. Some 17 percent of police officers are assaulted every year, 83 percent with personal weapons such as hands and feet. There are no data on assaults on security officers, but the consensus among trainers is that assaults on security officers occur at least as often.

With this increase comes an increase in the number of civil actions brought against officers, mostly for excessive force. The original report on an incident must thoroughly explain your actions taken in response to escalating resistance against you. Courts perceive that a law enforcement officer is entitled to use one level of force higher than the aggressor.

PSYCHOLOGY OF CONFRONTATION

When challenged for being in an unauthorized location, a person becomes anxious. He or she may feel frustration at being discovered, or fear what the perceived consequences might be. The body prepares for action. The heart rate increases, butterflies flutter in the stomach, the mouth goes dry, vision focuses as if looking down a tunnel, skin may blanch, and breathing becomes shallow and rapid.

And the same things happen to you when you anticipate conflict.

You can't afford to lose control or become overly anxious. Take some deep breaths. Command your body to relax. When relaxed, you are better prepared to react.

DIVERSION TECHNIQUES

Get the subject talking. When talking, the subject is not acting. Don't box the subject into a corner or block the door, giving the impression of cornering the subject. Keep a couple of arms' lengths distance. Ask polite questions in a soft voice and listen to the replies. You might repeat the subject's responses to show you are listening. Ask questions that build on what you are told. Ask for clarification of points needing more detail. Keep the dialogue going.

If the subject is angry, direct the conversation to the past. "I feel that you were angry then because . . ." This helps to defuse the emotion. Use the subject's name when you ask a question to slow the pace down and personalize your relationship. If you want to move to a safer location, suggest, "Why don't we step over here?" Everything about your words and tone of voice should show compassion, relieve tension. A soft voice is believable.

When two subjects are shouting at each other, conflict is near. Separate them. Ask the louder one to approach you to explain the situation, and tell the other to stay in place. You want at least seven yards between them. Keep your voice low to induce the subject to speak quietly and listen to you.

BODY LANGUAGE

Consider this scene: An officer and his partner had separated the combatants in a domestic dispute. The husband and wife were beginning to settle down when a third officer arrived on the scene. He strode into the room, baton in one hand striking the open palm of his other hand, and demanded, "What's the problem here?"

And the fight started all over again.

According to Roland Ouellette of R.E.B. Security Training Inc.,"When you communicate with a subject, 85 to 90 percent of the message you deliver is nonverbal. Only 10 to 15 percent of your message is transmitted verbally." You can learn to use body language phenomena to your advantage.

Look for the instinctive signs that indicate what a subject is thinking. Raising the hands in front of the torso, lowering the eyes, bowing the head, a drop in voice level, and grooming gestures all denote submission.

Watch for body language that telegraphs action. For instance, a subject is standing with head and shoulders back, breathing is shallow and rapid, lips are tight, and movements are exaggerated. The subject is ready to commit violence.

An attack may be imminent when the subject's face goes white, a boxer's stance is assumed with fists cocked, along with glances at your baton. The subject's center of gravity will drop before a move is made. Look for that little dip that signals an immediate action.

Picture a Marine drill sergeant. He intimidates a recruit by moving in close. Notice his stance as he towers over the poor trainee. His hands are on his hips. His shoulders are back. His chin is raised. His voice is loud and commanding. All these gestures send signals of aggression. This may be how you want to appear when dealing with a juvenile who just snatched an elderly woman's purse.

You can see the difference in the message you send if your head is back or bowed, chin up or down, shoulders back or forward, arms folded or open. In each case, the first is authoritative and the second is supportive.

Think of various gestures and postures. Expanding the body into a rigid, erect stance elicits a hostile response. Contracting the body, relaxing, bowing the head, stooping the shoulders, and standing obliquely is often effective in forestalling violence. Another important consideration is that supportive postures put you in a much better defensive position than the authoritative stances.

EYE CONTACT

When you stare at the subject directly in the eyes, you are showing that you are the powerful authority. However, a direct stare is not likely to elicit cooperation. If you drop your gaze down to about the sternum, you reduce the power role and become more of a helpful ally.

This works just the opposite if you are listening to the subject. Looking straight in the eye makes you appear interested in what is being said; you are paying attention. If you look off in the distance, or avoid eye contact, you appear uninterested.

However, if a subject gives you a blank stare, as if off in never-never land, WATCH OUT! When someone wants to cut your throat, they mentally depersonalize you, as if you were simply a blade of grass in front of the mower.

PERSONAL SPACE

Did you ever notice that when a second person joins someone in an elevator the two will divide the space equally? If a third person enters, they will share the space in thirds. If someone enters a nearly full elevator and faces the rear, toward the other people, they all feel uncomfortable. "That's because your personal space extends farther to the front than it does to the rear," Ouellette says.

Every individual is circled by three rings of a size specific to that individual. For the security officer, the outermost is the alert zone. Next is the defense zone, an area in which an invader puts you on the defensive. The innermost ring, with a diameter about an arm's length plus one hand, is the attack zone, where an invader is likely to incite a reaction. Most instructors define the attack zone as four to six feet. A civilian might call these zones social, personal, and intimate.

When you are dealing with a citizen in a verbal situation, stay out of the attack zone. Don't invade a person's body space because you may precipitate aggression against you. Also, if you are that close, you are vulnerable to attack.

VERBAL COMMUNICATIONS

One of the most used but least trained tools of the trade is the human voice. It's the one tool you always have with you, and you use it more than any other piece of security equipment. With it you establish authority and take command of a situation. Verbalization is a force by which you exercise control.

In one case, a rookie had completed his training with a field training officer. During his first shift on his own, he was dispatched to "unknown trouble" at a market in the mall. He found people milling around when he arrived and, in his best command voice, asked what was happening. A bystander pointed to a person slipping into the crowd and said something about the subject causing trouble. The rookie called to the subject, "Excuse me, uh, hey you, uh, I want to . . . We got a complaint of . . ." He became rattled when he couldn't define the complaint. The subject paid no attention, of course. The rookie caught up with him and grabbed him by the shoulder. The subject, drunk and angry, turned with a knife in his hand and slashed at the officer. The blade sliced his jacket, glanced off his body armor, and cut his forearm.

In another case, officers responded to a domestic disturbance in an apartment complex. Several family members stood arguing in the front yard. Neighbors were leaning out of their windows. The officers separated the most agitated combatants. Suddenly one officer and a subject began to scuffle. The subject broke free and ran with the officer in pursuit. Cornered by a fence, the subject turned and a shot rang out. The subject dropped, wounded in the leg. The officer said he struggled with the subject over a handgun the man carried in his belt. When the subject ran, then turned to point the weapon, the officer fired.

A weapon was found where the man fell, but no one had seen it before the shooting. The family said the man never owned a gun. A BATF (Bureau of Alcohol, Tobacco and Firearms) trace proved negative. Witnesses said they saw the struggle, but didn't hear the officer say anything. They simply saw the officer chase the subject, draw his weapon and fire. They said they saw no weapon other than the officer's. This situation would have been clearly in the officer's favor if he had used his voice, "Drop that weapon!"

There are two very different lessons in these examples.

A COMMAND VOICE

Short, loud commands elicit quick obedience (remember the Marine drill instructor). A person under stress will focus on the few action words. Lengthy verbiage is superfluous and counterproductive.

Words that begin with a hard consonant, an explosive rush of air, are more effective than those with a soft sound. "Stop" is better than "Halt." "Don't move" is better than "Stand still."

First, identify yourself. "Security!" That establishes your identity and authority. Say it even if you're in uniform, the suspect and witnesses may be looking somewhere else.

Second, issue a terse, loud, lawful command that people are predisposed to obey. Imagine you are walking among some rocks on a sunny summer day and your buddy yells, "Don't move!" You would freeze in your tracks, even if you didn't hear the rattle of a snake just two steps ahead. When we were toddlers, we learned to obey those short, loud, one-word commands from our mothers.

Project your voice the way an actor does on stage. When you shout "Security," your abdominal muscles should contract to push air from the bottom of your lungs. Stage actors describe it as talking from the diaphragm. It adds volume and distance with surprisingly little extra effort. In the first example, perhaps the man would have stopped, and the officer would not have been slashed, if the officer had shouted "Stop!"

During interviews, offenders have indicated they do not try to resist or evade officers whose bearing indicates they are in control of the situation. Officers who act hesitant or uncertain, like the officer in the first example, are the ones offenders ignore, escape from, or even attack.

EXTENDING COMMANDS

Once you have identified yourself and the subject has stopped, clearly and loudly tell the subject what to do next. In the second example, the officer said nothing and the witnesses heard nothing. Suppose the officer had shouted, "Stop!" Perhaps the suspect would have, perhaps not. But if the officer had added three little words—"Drop that weapon!"—it would have helped to establish the fact that the subject was armed, even if the witnesses didn't see the gun.

The U.S. Supreme Court specifically states in the *Tennessee v. Garner (1985)* decision that verbal commands must be given whenever practical. This same decision also negates the threat "Stop or I'll shoot." The suspect knows that you can't shoot if no one is being threatened. An empty threat makes you look foolish if your bluff is called. If the situation is such that you have your gun in your hand, it's better to explain to the suspect, "Don't do anything that would force me to shoot you."

GIVING COMMANDS

Your response is determined by how the suspect reacts. Remember, the suspect cannot comply unless your command is heard. Use the fewest hard consonant words possible to deliver commands: "Put your hands up!" "Drop to the ground! Face down." "Show me your hands! Slowly." "Turn around!" "Face the wall!"

Upon compliance, these commands move the suspect into a controlled and safe position. They establish that you are in control. If the suspect doesn't obey, reinforce the commands with "Do it now!" in a loud voice.

If the suspect still doesn't comply, escalate the use of force. Continue talking, however. It may ease the resistance when you apply a pain compliance technique. For example, you could say, "Cooperate with me and there will be no pain."

An equally important element of verbalization is talking to your partner about what is occurring. If you lose control of an aggressive subject's arm, your partner needs to know that.

DEBRIEFING

Verbalization doesn't end with the capture. Debrief the suspect. "Are you all right? I notice you hit your head. Do you need a doctor?"

This gives you time to get your own thoughts together, catch your breath, and regain physical control. By that time, you may have an audience. These questions demonstrate to witnesses your concern for the subject's well-being—and they can testify to that fact.

Consider the four D's: dialogue, direction, debriefing, and documentation.

Dialogue refers to communicating your actions to your partner. Direction refers to your commands, make it clear that the subject understood them. Debriefing can mean showing concern for the well-being of the subject, especially if the use of force was required. Once the apprehension is made, document your actions throughout the event. Cite the subject's actions that compelled your reactions.

Chapter 12
THREAT RESPONSE

A security officer may have to use as much force as is reasonable and necessary to accomplish a legitimate objective. Remember those two words. If you can employ simple procedures to exert control over a subject, you won't need to resort to impact weapons or more forceful devices. But it's not a black and white picture—the graduated use of degrees of force passes through many shades of gray, depending on the threat. Officers must instinctively know the appropriate responses between the extremes of a polite request and pulling the trigger. When a defensive tactic can avoid the ultimate defensive force, it's a better choice.

Things to consider in responding to force, or forcing compliance, include:

Threat—is the subject threatening you with a weapon of some sort?

Resistance—is the subject resisting your lawful order?

Physical comparison—is the subject much weaker or stronger than you? An officer should not need to use as much force to gain the compliance of a petite female as for a large male, even if the officer is a petite female.

Prior behavior—was the subject belligerent or submissive prior to the time your order was given? Once a subject realizes you mean business, a belligerent antagonist can suddenly become quite submissive—or vice versa.

It is better to grip a reluctant subject's arm convincingly to gain compliance rather than using the baton. A physical response is likely to induce more aggression, more injuries, and greater potential for civil suit. You may be able to resolve a situation with a simple grip that causes pain, avoiding a knock-down, drag-out fight.

There's also a very practical reason for keeping the response level low. As the level of your response increases, so do the chances for a lawsuit. When you pull your gun and fire, it means that all other control techniques were inappropriate, or were tried and failed. It means that the only way you could stop the aggressor's felonious assault was to shoot before death or grievous bodily harm occurred.

CONTINUUM OF FORCE

Threat response is a continuum of graduated use of force dictated by the subject's degree of resistance. Remember—your use of force must always be as a response.

At the bottom of the ladder, your presence on a scene is a forceful influence. Your stance and the image you project can influence a situation. Put your hands on your hips and stick your nose in the air, you will exude dominance. Stand relaxed with chin down, you will appear supportive.

When speaking to a suspect you are exercising oral control, a form of force dependent on your tone of voice. Verbal force begins with your request to a subject. It progresses to an order, then to an ORDER! Finally, you explain the consequences if the subject doesn't comply with your polite demands. These are the successive rungs as you work your way up the ladder of force.

By touching a subject you have initiated the next level of force—unarmed defensive control techniques. These include an unobtrusive grab of the subject's arm that appears passive, but gives you a measure of control, as when walking a suspect from a position of advantage. It can escalate to a pain compliance technique, such as a wrist or thumb lock.

Higher up the ladder are the impact weapons. Your weapon may be as passive as a short stick on your key ring. When you know how to use it, that short stick may enable you to control someone much stronger than you. The baton is seen by the public as a standard piece of equipment, ranging from a 26-inch stick carried on patrol to the 36-inch riot baton which looks more threatening. Nonlethal weapons, including chemical agents and electronic devices, escalate the level of force.

Finally, the outer limit of the continuum is the response of deadly force against the threat of deadly force.

When lethal force is justified, you think first of the gun. That's the usual response to a deadly threat. But consider this: Any force you apply that results in death is deadly force. If you strike a suspect's head with your baton and the suspect dies from a brain concussion, that's deadly force. If you apply a bar arm choke hold on a struggling suspect who then suffocates, that's deadly force.

Of course, different devices are perceived differently. Your baton is considered nonlethal even though you can easily kill someone with it. Your gun is considered lethal even though only one in five police shootings results in death. The term deadly force refers to the result rather than the tool.

The officer-in-training has positioned her weight and used a wristlock to prevent the subject from getting up. *(Dave Thorstenson)*

APPROPRIATE RESPONSE

As a security officer, you are concerned with the application of force appropriate to the threat. Remember, you will have to explain your actions in court. Invariably, the court will use "reasonable force" in judging a complaint. According to police trainer Massad Ayoob, "the judgment of the reasonable man" is a standard of the American legal system. Each case is decided on its own extenuating circumstances. That's why properly presented truth is your strongest weapon in court.

Your job is protecting your employer's assets, personnel, and visitors. If a thief puts the potted plant from the lobby down and makes a beeline for the door, the threat to your employer's property is over. It may be better to let the offender go. It's not your job to enforce society's laws. But if he drops the plant and lunges at you, then a new threat begins.

Remember that the twin objectives of the use of force are to achieve control and then maintain that control. The force of the response must be appropriate to the level of resistance or aggression exerted against you.

If you tell the subject in an authoritative voice to leave the premises and he just stands there, your level of force is ineffective. It puts you in jeopardy of losing control of the situation. If a subject curses you and you zap him with a stun gun to punish him, that's excessive force. You are justified in using only the level of force necessary to resolve the situation.

WHEN TO BACK OFF

Another part of threat response training is knowing the difference between backing off and backing down.

If you know the subject is a skilled fighter with an aggressive personality, you may have to rapidly escalate to a high level of force to resolve the situation. In a circumstance like this, it makes more sense to back off and try to defuse the situation—providing it doesn't expose others to injury.

If you are facing a deadly force situation with no chance of winning, do not proceed. Don't be like the person who brought a knife to a gun fight. When you cannot control a subject or a situation, de-escalate your response. Disengage, step back, and move to cover to wait for backup. Then become a trained witness, reporting information, noting details and descriptions.

Proper threat response encompasses a wide variety of actions, ranging through a continuum of body language, verbalization, commands, passive restraints, active countermeasures, nonlethal weapons, and firearms. An overemphasis on any one part of this continuum puts the officer at a disadvantage, leaving fewer alternatives.

STREET WEAPONS SURPRISE YOU

Be aware that guns, slicers, push knives, and pointy things you do not recognize as weapons can be used against you. Potentially lethal weapons may look no more threatening than a belt buckle, pen, necklace, wallet, fanny pack, or umbrella. Some you can learn to recognize. Some you may not see in time, unless you read the body language of the suspect.

Furtive eye movements or a sweep of the hand over a belt buckle or pocket can signal an impending attack. Remember that even a small knife can be significant. Emergency room physicians attest that just three millimeters of penetration into an area like the neck can be fatal.

COMPLACENCY IS DEADLY

The greatest single threat to a security officer is complacency. Avoid the routine, be alert, remain in at least condition yellow at all times. One training film shows officers responding to a bank alarm for the umpteenth time. It had been a false alarm each time before, so the officers were complacent. They were discussing where to go fishing for the weekend when the robber came out of the bank and killed both of them with a shotgun.

A call goes out for, perhaps, two officers to respond to a disturbance caused by the company troublemaker. During numerous previous incidents, the subject never resisted. No one got hurt. The subject was placed in custody and everyone took an assist on their log.

Perhaps this time the subject is fed up with being hassled by security, or thinks the judge is likely to put him away. You cannot be certain of how a person will react, even if the reaction was compliant a thousand times before. If you anticipate compliance you could be injured or killed when surprised by an attack.

OFFICER IN CHARGE

Any time two or more officers are involved in the same situation, one must take charge. Even though there are no sergeant stripes on your sleeve, if the dispatcher sent you, you are in charge. Your planning must be more than "You take the back and I'll go in the front."

For instance, a suspect in a house must be detained. You need to contain the suspect and maintain the status quo. Two officers can watch all sides of a house when they are at opposite corners. If other officers are assigned to a containment position, they must not leave that position unless relieved or cleared. Otherwise, the offender can escape through your abandoned position.

First, assign officers to watch other avenues of possible attack. Then, project the next move if the subject slams the door in your face or attacks. Once in position, decide who will execute the handcuffing.

Consider the alternative and you'll see why I include "Officer in Charge" under use of force. If six officers surround an area and each acts independently of the others, who knows what each is doing? If the subject attacks one of six independent officers, how would you like to be the one wrestling around on the floor while five excited officers point guns at the two of you? If there is no officer in charge, who is watching others in the area? Or covering the back of the officer involved in the scuffle?

A scenario such as this should be a "snatch and grab." Do not remain on the scene unnecessarily after the suspect is detained. Once you have departed, any resistance or belligerent assistance from friends of the subject will end.

Complacency, familiarity, and routine are the deadly enemies.

Consider another scenario: A female stenographer employed by your company is estranged from her husband and has a restraining order to keep him away. He shows up at the office and walks past you. With knowledge of the restraining order, you may use the force necessary to prevent the husband from violating the court order. Estranged wives have been murdered with restraining orders in their purses.

In any situation where force must be used, you can count on the aggrieved filing civil suit against you. If you get into a fight, consider calling police and filing a complaint against the assailant. Remember, you never start a fight. You are always the aggrieved party.

What if you respond to an attack against you, and the attacker suddenly stops the attack? You must stop the response. If you continue to pelt the person with your baton, you become the attacker. Also, be aware that for the security officer, "stepping outside" to settle matters is not acceptable. There is no legal defense against such a combat, even if agreed to by the other party.

We have emphasized the use of force in protection of persons. What about protection of premises or property?

What is the response if an employee is walking away with the company president's stereo? Suppose the employee says, "I loaned this unit to the company and I want it back." If the employee has a legitimate claim, there's no crime and you are not authorized to use force. Of course, you may detain the employee while you check the story to confirm ownership.

OFFICER SURVIVAL

Survival is a frame of mind. When approaching a scene, do so in a manner that will allow you to survive if something goes wrong. For instance, when searching an area for an armed adversary, use techniques that minimize your exposure to danger. Wear your body armor on patrol. Maintain your equipment so it will function when needed. Survival is simply a matter of doing everything right.

One of the biggest threats to officer safety is relaxing prematurely. Even a handcuffed subject can swing a baseball bat. An officer assigned to guard suspects should have no other duties or distractions.

Survival means being aware of the little signs that signal danger, being alert, knowing what you're up against. To improve the odds, identify and evaluate potentially hazardous situations and critical areas. Identify the dangers presented during past cases: ambushes, barricaded subjects, hostage situations, vehicle stops. Identify the signs and signals that warrant concern. Develop a survivor's attitude.

Many of us maintain the attitude that "It'll never happen to me." It's not a question of *if* you will ever confront a serious situation requiring a drastic response. It's a matter of *when*. Develop an attitude of watching for and expecting the worst while dealing politely with people and remaining ready to act. You will be well on your way to being a survivor.

Chapter 13
DEFENSIVE TECHNIQUES

Defensive tactics—the proper physical, unarmed response to resistance—are vitally important. A lack of these skills can cut your career short, allowing you to fail against an aggressor or to respond with "excessive force." You cannot learn the techniques discussed here simply by reading. You must learn from a hands-on approach under the guidance of a qualified instructor.

Note that your responses throughout this chapter are prompted by the level of force exerted against you. Think of the use of defensive techniques as a continuum of force, a ladder with rungs labeled from "verbal order" at the bottom to "deadly force" at the top. Because you are the representative of authority, courts accept that you must use slightly more force than the level exerted against you in order to carry out your mission.

The use of force slides up and down the scale. If someone passively refuses to do what you say, you may have to push a bit. If a subject takes a swing at you, you deflect it and get into an arm lock to prevent further aggression. If the subject pulls a knife and threatens you, you resort to the weapons available.

However, it's a two-way ladder. For example, an adult male aggressor swings a piece of lead pipe at your head. You parry it with your baton. Then he drops it and holds out his wrists for cuffing. Do you bash him with your baton? Of course not. As he reduces his level of force, so do you, always retaining the potential of escalating again if he does.

COMPLIANCE HOLDS

The subjects you face in a confrontation will be in one of three frames of mind. The "yes" person is compliant, showing identification and getting out of the car when asked. A cooperative subject will drop a gun when covered.

The "no" person resists, tells you to commit an unnatural act on yourself, and takes a combative stance, indicating a readiness to fight. This person must be dealt with in a more forceful manner.

Then there's the "maybe" person, the passive resister who is debating whether to comply, fight, or run.

Compliance holds are applicable to the "maybe" person. They may be used when you feel you have an advantage in size, strength, skill, or backup support. They're intended to help convince the subject to do what you want.

BLANKET HOLD

If the subject is passive, grasp the right elbow with both of your hands, thumbs up. Most people are right-handed. It's safer if two officers each take one arm, but, if you're alone, odds are the right is the strong side. This is a gentle grasp that gives you good control of the arm. The subject can't elbow you or backhand you. If the subject tries to run at that point, slip into the escort position.

ESCORT POSITION

Slide your right hand down to the suspect's wrist and get a good pincer grip between your thumb and middle finger. The opposing thumb and middle finger make the hand's strongest grip. Bring the subject's elbow close to your center, as you continue the grip on the elbow.

There are variations of the escort position. Some recommend twisting the hand under, so the back of the hand is against your hip, and hooking your other thumb under the subject's armpit. Some don't recommend this because the subject may drop a shoulder down from your left hand or, if double jointed, bend an elbow. In any case, you lose control.

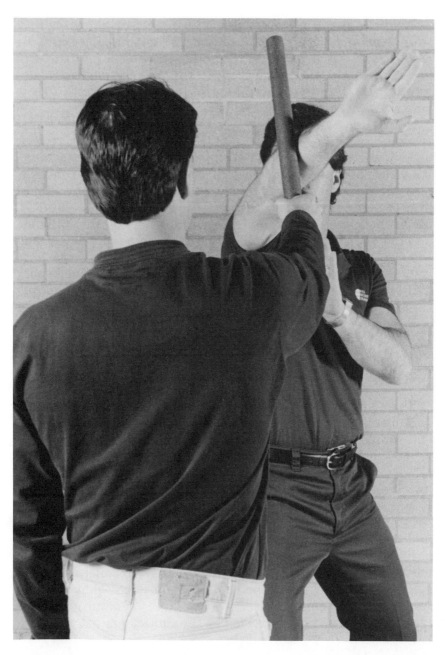

Within the continuum of force—if an assailant swings at you, first deflect it and then use an arm lock to prevent further aggression. *(Dave Thorstenson)*

For instance, you are holding the subject's right arm, with your left hand on his elbow and your right hand locking his wrist. He starts to resist. When you quickly bend forward with force, what do you think happens to the subject? He goes forward. Let him to the ground gently; you don't want to write long reports explaining any injuries.

Notice that this scenario gives you a sequence of events that you can explain in your report as justification for the increasing use of forceful measures. Control is not a fifty-fifty proposition. It's all or nothing. If you have half control, you have no control.

While this escalation is taking place, keep telling the subject in a commanding voice, "Sir, calm down. Don't hurt yourself. Stop resisting. Drop the knife. Don't make me do this." Should he grab your holstered gun, as you chop his hand away, shout, "Sir, let go the gun!" Your explosive verbalization adds force to your chop, and lets witnesses know the subject threatened you.

If you lose control, duck behind the subject to where he can't reach you. Then create distance, so you can draw your baton or gun.

COME-ALONG HOLDS

There are many variations of come-alongs, applied with either both hands, one hand, or a baton. However, they all boil down to one simple principle. Anchor the subject's elbow and bend his wrist—the common wrist lock. Any way you can anchor his elbow and bend his hand down with your force against his knuckles, you've got control.

I've seen come-along holds applied in many ways, but the point is to jam the elbow into your lower chest, grab his hand, and bend it down. Depending on the pressure you exert, it's either a come-along or pain compliance technique to "stabilize" a person and encourage cooperation. It's part of an overall system—the steps along the continuum of force—that can flow from a gentle touch to excruciating pain, depending on the resistance or aggression exerted by the subject against you.

PRESSURE POINT CONTROL

Pressure-point control has graduated from a distraction technique to a system which provides a high degree of control. It requires little skill, strength, or size to be effective and takes little effort on the part of the officer.

An anatomy book shows many points on the body where nerves, bones, and muscular hollows are situated so as to be vulnerable. While these are points to which many of the defensive techniques with a short stick or baton are directed, some are vulnerable to your hand.

Bruce Siddle of PPCT Management Systems has probably studied pressure-point control more than anyone. What he can do with what appears to be a simple grab is astonishing. This could be quite a technical medical subject, but he makes it simple—something you and I can do.

TOUCH PRESSURE POINTS

There are many places where a forceful touch can induce pain. One is the inside of the upper arm between the biceps and triceps muscles. Another is the muscle leading from shoulder to neck—place fingers or thumb into the depression above the collarbone and opposing digits on the other side, and squeeze. Touch pressure points are best used on "maybe" people, so they are a form of come-along. If you can't get the wrist, a one-hand hold at a touch pressure point may do the trick.

THREE POINTS FOR QUICK PENETRATION

When a subject actively resists, you need to grab a pressure point that quickly convinces him to do what you ask. There are many potential points of vulnerability, but what can you grab in a fight? What can you get to quickly and surely? How many different holds can you remember? The experts emphasize three accessible points: behind the ear, beneath the jaw, and at the base of the neck.

To find these points instinctively, you must be personally trained by a qualified instructor and experience the exercises.

PAIN COMPLIANCE

Pain compliance is an alternative technique, but it is not a sure thing. Different people have different tolerances for pain. A subject high on drugs may not feel pain and your technique may not work. When it fails, by definition, the subject is no longer a "maybe" person. You are dealing with a "no" person that requires force higher up on the continuum—and you may have to explain to the judge why you had to use a higher level of force to gain compliance.

There is much misunderstanding about pain compliance restraints involving the neck. It is important to be informed of the facts.

LATERAL VASCULAR NECK RESTRAINTS

When you are facing a husky adversary, especially one that's larger than you, technique rather than brute strength is required.

I once saw a film of a 125-pound female police officer restrain, take down, and cuff a 210-pound construction worker. She started with a kick into the backs of his knees. Then, she got her arm all the way around the worker's neck. Her elbow was in front and her hand extended back behind his shoulder. Her other hand came up and clasped that hand, palms together with fingers wrapped, not interlaced. Then she pulled. Her hip hit the worker's buttocks, broke his balance to the rear, and she had him under control.

She was using the lateral vascular neck restraint, originated by Jim Lindell, physical training instructor for the Kansas City, Missouri, police and third-degree black belt in judo. This system was developed to control violent subjects. It's not a combat tactic. One basic hold can be applied with three levels of effect (you rarely need the third level). And it eliminates the hazards of the old choke hold.

DANGER OF THE BAR ARM CHOKE HOLD

With all the publicity given to liability suits lost after a perpetrator died as a result of being restrained by a choke hold, only a reminder should be needed here. But, incredibly, I hear that some police are still being taught the bar arm hold. Let this be a word to the wise: Never use a bar-arm choke hold.

A bar across the front of a subject's neck—whether it's your forearm, flashlight, or baton—can damage the windpipe, break the hyoid bone (Adam's apple), crush the larynx (voice box), and bring dire consequences to both you and the subject. You are justified in using only the degree of force necessary to effect the arrest. If the suspect dies, you used deadly force, whether you meant to or not.

In a reverse situation, when an aggressor puts his arm around your neck, get your chin into the crook of his elbow immediately. You are avoiding a bar arm and protecting your airway. You need to understand the danger of a hold on someone's neck.

ACTIVE COUNTERMEASURES

Lt. Gary Klugiewicz, defensive tactics coordinator for the Milwaukee County, Wisconsin, sheriff's department recruit training academy, is nationally known for his Active Countermeasures course. It's a system of blocks, punches, and kicks that turn violent resistance into control. Of course, Gary makes it look easy. He's a third-degree black belt in United States Kyokushin karate and placed ninth in world-class competition in Japan. The class is taught by demonstration, explanation, and repetition—realistic simulations. He puts students through the exercises and drills to ensure they are well-practiced in performing the techniques.

Realistic simulation is important. If you ever received defensive tactics training in an academy, the instructor probably warned you about breaking your partner's finger. You had to hold back, indicating where you'd strike with the baton, rather than actually striking. The minute your partner felt pain, he or she slapped twice—the universal martial arts signal to stop. The techniques you were learning could potentially do damage to the person on whom you applied them.

DECENTRALIZATIONS

In court, you refer to "decentralizing" the subject. "Takedown" is cop talk. When a subject actively resists or attacks, he's not cooperating; he's a "no" person. He isn't going to voluntarily assume a handcuffing position. You have to put him there.

Like most defensive tactics, there are different techniques, variations on a theme. But a takedown—decentralization—must provide for the safety of the subject by protecting his head and neck and controlling the speed of descent. It must work whether you do it fast or slow. Grabbing a subject's hair or head and twisting him to the ground may give you control of his head, but this move can cause whiplash to the neck.

An obnoxious drunk would be "directed" to the ground more carefully and slowly than someone trying to resist. But you still must know how to do it right. If you use a full body slam and smash his face into the concrete so hard he breaks his neck and dies, the court will call it deadly force. Not only does that open a whole new concern in justifying your actions, but your conscience must live with it for the rest of your life.

These techniques must also be practical. The classic rearward takedown is probably still being taught in many places, but Klugiewicz found that it wasn't being used on the street. It might work when done fast, but it didn't work when done slowly. He dropped it from the curriculum.

Now Klugiewicz teaches one basic principle that satisfies the above requirements and works from whatever grip you have on a subject. The application can be hard or soft, fast or slow. When the subject is off balance, you can stop halfway for safety. Simply bring the subject to your center and bend over as if you were reaching for your right foot with your left hand (assuming you've got his right arm).

THREE LEVELS

The secret of delivering a forceful blow is to translate force through fluid shock waves to motor points of the body. A punch, for example, doesn't stop on contact. To demonstrate, Klugiewicz had me hold my left arm out and hit the mound of my forearm with my right open hand. It looked like a karate chop, retracting immediately. "Everybody hits like that," according to Klugiewicz. "There's no power. This time secure your arm by putting it on the table, and hit it again, but let it sink in." What a difference. My arm hurt.

A boxing parallel might be the difference between a jab and a punch. Rather than pulling back, you imagine the target a bit beyond where your fist hits. You want to transfer the kinetic energy from your hand through fluid shock waves to the subject's internal functions. It's the same principle with a bullet or a baton.

STUNNING TECHNIQUE

When someone grapples with you, that is an assault. Remember to call it an assault. Can you strike him? Of course. But, what if the subject is hyped up, drunk, or emotionally upset? If you punch him once in the head, it probably won't do any good. You need to divert the subject's attention, take away the ability to resist. "I 'direct' him to a wall, squad car, tree, bridge abutment—any hard object," Klugiewicz explains.

BODY SLAM

When someone slams into a hard object, the impact creates a dysfunction. It can knock the wind out of someone. When a subject hits a wall backwards, it causes a spread-out diffused strike, disrupting the synapses of the brain. Try it yourself during a training session with a qualified instructor: Stand about four inches from the wall and ask your partner to push you forcefully backward. When the back of your shoulders hits the wall, your eyes stutter and you feel shaken.

With one well-placed blow that will cause no permanent damage, you have accomplished more than multiple blows with your portable radio or baton could have produced. "We found that many officers have done this instinctively," Klugiewicz says. "And you can do it vertically or horizontally with a much lower propensity for damage."

DIFFUSED STRIKE

Using fluid shock waves to cause trauma to the body, you can addle a subject without really causing harm. If you break his bones, you'll have to write a long report. You want to hit the places where it won't cause serious damage.

Klugiewicz laid the inside of his forearm at the base of my neck, the same place we discussed in pressure point control. Then he pulled his arm out six to eight inches and slammed it back with modest force. That was enough to cause some discomfort.

"This diffused strike is like a mobile wall stun," he explains. It's not like a chop-and-retract that does little, or punching "through" that pushes the subject backward. When you do it right, you can feel the vibration in the subject's body. It's comparable to the energy dump of an expanding bullet going into ballistic gelatin. "You don't need a lot of techniques or a high skill level if you learn to hit properly using fluid shock waves," Klugiewicz adds.

UNARMED BLOCKING AND STRIKING

When attacked, assume a ready position like a boxer's stance—hands up by your face, elbows tucked in. Swing side to side to guard against chest attacks. If the subject swings high, pop your arm up, block, and retract. Abdominal strikes can be deflected by dropping your elbow. If the subject swings low, swoop your arm down, around, and back up.

Don't stand there and box. Your purpose is to end the confrontation as quickly as possible. One block is all you should need. Once you have blocked an attack, counterattack with a hand or leg strike, wrist lock, diffused strike, baton, or gun—whatever is called for.

A vertical punch to the suspect's jaw (like a left jab with the fist held vertically) stops any forward momentum, causes the subject to bring his hands up, and sets him up for a reverse punch (like a strong right punch) to the lower abdomen to stun him. Then you can direct him to the ground and cuff him, effecting control with a minimum amount of force.

Besides the fists, you can block or strike with the forearm, front or back side of the elbow, knee, or foot. A front kick aimed at the lower abdomen may keep the subject away. If he's already too close, put your knee into his abdomen. This is always effective.

PURPOSES

Active countermeasures are defensive techniques used when an officer can't reach the baton or firearm, or to regain lost control. They provide you with a "weapon" to use when the situation is no longer appropriate for impact weapons.

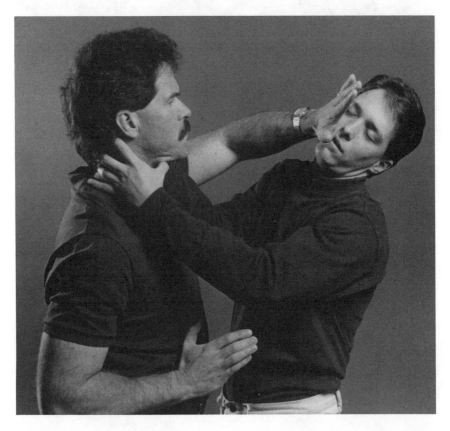

Active countermeasures are defensive techniques used when the officer can't reach the baton or firearm, or to regain lost control. *(Dave Thorstenson)*

A front kick aimed at the lower abdomen will move an attacker away from you.

Active countermeasures serve as a defense against an assault. They can distract the assailant. They can stun and disorient the subject, or impede him when his legs are knocked out from under him. They can stop an attack. They can enable you to control an aggressive subject and manage him into a position where he can no longer threaten you.

Klugiewicz employs very few fundamentals in his active countermeasures system. "We don't want multiple techniques that you won't remember," he explains. "We want multiple applications of a few effective techniques you will remember."

Chapter 14
DEFENSIVE DEVICES

The security officer is given authority beyond what the law allows the average citizen. You are allowed to impose your will on an uncooperative subject who is violating the law or company rules. Because of this, you may be exempt from legislative prohibitions against certain weapons.

There are many devices on the market. You can't evaluate the need for such items unless you understand something about them. You will probably be issued a baton, although some companies don't use them. You'll need a flashlight, but what kind? Saps or blackjacks may still be found in the hands of old-timers. The following broad categories will give you an understanding of the variety of devices available.

HUMANE DEVICES

Society is constantly looking for ways to restrain a subject without causing harmful effects. Tear gas was developed in World War I; the rubber bullets used in Northern Ireland are an attempt at "humane" riot control. This search has produced a variety of devices designed for an officer's personal use, but a truly humane, effective device has yet to be found.

For the officer trained in defensive tactics, most nonlethal devices are unnecessary "crutches." They may be of help to officers less confident in their physical skills, and some are designed to work against multiple adversaries.

For instance, consider an unarmed but violent mental patient, or a person under the influence of hallucinogenic drugs. You don't want to kill someone like this, but you must get the person under control. Captur-Net uses the technique of the fisherman who tosses a round purse seine over a school of minnows to capture the bait; two officers can fling a net over a subject to entangle and subdue him.

The stun grenade creates a loud bang and bright flash with no harmful shrapnel. It serves the purpose in tactical situations of distracting and disorienting a perpetrator.

ELECTRICAL DEVICES

Of numerous electrical devices used by enforcement agencies, stun guns have been in the news in recent years, usually under an unfavorable light. The Source, which is no longer manufactured, included a flashlight on one end and short electrodes on the other. When it was pressed against an aggressive subject and turned on, the pain-producing shock caused a reactive reflex. The Nova XR5000 is designed to incapacitate a combative subject by inducing muscle spasms. It produces a high-voltage current that causes loss of muscular control, leaving the subject dazed but conscious.

CHEMICAL DEVICES

The U.S. Army expended numerous resources developing an inoffensive chemical agent suitable for training troops in the use of gas masks during World War I. The result was Chloraceteophenone, or CN. This is tear gas, a lacrimating (tear-causing) agent. It's not really a gas, but a fine powder "dust" in a carrier, such as smoke in a grenade or liquid in an aerosol container. When a person is exposed to it, the tear ducts flow, the eyes smart, and the eyelids try to close. A burning sensation is felt on moist skin. Once removed from the gas, the effects soon dissipate. There are no adverse after-effects and it's relatively easy to clean up an area after exposure.

In 1960, the Army adopted a new chemical agent called Orthochlorbenzalmalonontrile. Remember it as CS. CS is a more potent irritant, more effective than CN against a mob. The effects of CS include an extreme burning sensation and involuntary closure of the eyes, flowing tears, coughing and chest tightening, sinus and nasal drip, and extreme burning sensations on areas of moist skin such as the face, armpits, and groin. If used indoors, CS is more difficult to clean up than CN.

All chemical-agent devices are color coded. Red is CN, blue is CS, yellow is HC or smoke, green is DM, and grey indicates practice items. Violet is CR, a new chemical agent not used in the United States. You probably will never use DM, which is a sickening agent used by the military. The two you are most likely to see are CN (red) and CS (blue).

A different characteristic becomes important when you put these substances into an aerosol container.

AEROSOL SPRAYS

When the controversy over "Chemical Mace" made national news, I witnessed some tests and read reports of other law enforcement agencies that evaluated a variety of aerosol devices. They all reached similar conclusions. CN vaporizes much more readily than CS, hence, the milder of the two produces a quicker reaction when sprayed in a stream into an aggressor's face. From among the various manufacturers, you can get either CN or CS in an aerosol device.

Today, my choice of an aerosol spray would be a formula of oleoresin capsicum (OC) sold under a variety of trade names. Cap-stun is the more prominent, but you'll also find Punch, PepperMace and other brands on the market.

These products use a proprietary formulation of tincture of oleoresin capsicum (OC), or dissolved cayenne pepper, as its active ingredient. It works. I attended an instructor class for the Cap-Stun OC device. Volunteers in the class were sprayed with one percent solution Cap-Stun. My eyes immediately closed. Some class members had fits of uncontrollable coughing. You feel disoriented and confused. Any fight is forgotten. It took ten minutes of splashing cold water on my face before I could blink my eyes open long enough to flush out the OC.

OC is not considered a chemical agent. A research chemist with the FBI Forensic Science Research and Training Center and an analytical chemist with the Human Investigations Committee have stated that OC is outside of regulatory guidelines applicable to synthetic chemical agents, such as CS and CN.

This training class "volunteered" to show the effectiveness of the new Cap-Stun OC spray against an unruly crowd. *(Dave Thorstenson)*

OC is an inflammatory agent, rather than a lacrimating agent like CN. It is a solution, rather than a particulate. Decontamination procedures recommended are evaporation and flushing with cool water. Subjects do not require medical attention after exposure to OC. After extensive research by the FBI's Firearms Training Unit, no harmful side or after-effects have been identified with the use of OC.

For these reasons, trainers place OC into the force continuum below the active takedowns and pain compliance holds. Tear gas aerosols are next above pain compliance holds, followed by impact weapons and "deadly" force.

FIRST AID

It is likely that your company policy dictates that if you gas someone, you must provide first aid. Fortunately, common sense practices apply to OC, CN, and CS.

Remove the subject to a clear area, face into the wind. Don't let the subject rub or scratch. This only pushes the particulate deeper into the skin. This treatment is sufficient if exposure isn't severe. Flushing the eyes with cool, clear water will speed recovery, but use ten times more water than seems necessary. Always remove contact lenses before flushing the eyes.

If clothes have become contaminated, remove them. But be careful; you can pick up the agent on your hands and contaminate yourself. Normal cleaning will restore clothing. Don't use any creams, salves, or dressings on irritated skin. They trap the agent and prolong its effects.

Exposure to aerosol sprays creates a psychological effect on normal people—it seems you can't get your breath. If someone shows signs of severe or prolonged effects such as difficulty with breathing, severe chest pain, or contamination of wounds, get medical help.

SHORT STICK

Yawara, as an art, dates back to 17th-century Japan. Jujitsu schools of that time included the short stick among its weapons, with tactics so fierce it became known as "seven inches of sudden death."

Such severe martial arts tactics and weapons have no place in security service. Although you may use the Yawara strictly as a defensive weapon, it is perceived by the public as a martial arts device. Defensive techniques have evolved from the Yawara, however, that appear to be less intimidating. The short stick is not referred to as a Yawara in this text.

Most Yawaras today are made either with rounded ends or with a steel ball on each end. More than a dozen varying designs have been popular over the years, although all have a relatively thick grip limiting the techniques to thrusting, striking, or blocking.

It isn't unusual to put a fob of some kind on your key ring. A short stick is a handy device that you can tuck into your belt and keep the keys safe and accessible. The restroom key at the gasoline station is usually on a stick so customers don't lose it; this is the same idea.

Why would you want to keep your keys on a short stick? Let me tell you a story.

A DEFENSIBLE DEFENSIVE DEVICE

When I attended a Kubotan instructor course at the Smith & Wesson Academy, John Peters of the Defensive Tactics Institute told the story of an officer who was sued for brutality after taking down a particularly boisterous resister. The judge told the officer to bring the weapon he used into court. When the officer appeared the next day, the judge didn't see anything in his hands and became irritated.

"Where's your weapon?" the judge demanded angrily. "Did you bring it?"

"Yes, I did, your honor," the officer replied. "Well, let me see it."

With that, the officer put his key ring on the table. It had a six-inch stick on it, with six grooves that apparently provided a grip. When the officer explained that this indeed was the weapon he used to subdue the aggressor, the judge used colorful language in throwing the case out of court.

WHY IT WORKS

The short stick is a pain compliance device in police use. There are a number of points on the body where the bone is close under the skin and pressure against the resistant bone with a hard object produces pain. Like other pain compliance techniques, the short stick isn't an absolute solution. It's an alternative to more severe force, and it may work in certain situations.

Six basic techniques are taught, all of which are variations of two simple moves: a squeeze and a poke. There are numerous methods and situations in which short-stick principles are applied.

For instance, the edge of the stick under a protester's ear lobe will convince him to sit up. Or if a motorist gets a death grip on the steering wheel and refuses to leave the car, slip the stick over the wrist and step back as you grind the stick into the radial bone.

If someone grabs you in a bear hug from behind, you have several options. Bounce your head into their face. Swing your hip out of the way, as you chop your hand or stick down and back into the groin. If you can't move your upper arms, use a pen from your shirt pocket or short stick from your belt to poke the back of the assailant's hand. If you're in a full-Nelson hold, you can still reach the back of the subject's hand. As the grip loosens, swing the stick into the lower abdomen. If you're in a choke hold, tuck your chin into the crook of the subject's elbow to protect your airway and poke the stick into the muscles and tendons of the forearm. The short stick isn't an impact weapon, but if someone kicks at you, you can sidestep as you snap it down onto a shin.

With this technique, the short stick can be an effective tool in dealing with unarmed combatants. Then, if you are accused of using excessive force, the judge will not be inclined to rule harshly based on the contents of your key ring.

IMPACT WEAPONS

When Sir Robert Peel established the world's first organized police force in London in 1829, he armed the officers with truncheons, a stick that has carried over into the New World as the police baton. The baton has always been part of police equipment. History classifies the baton as an impact weapon, but police do not use it that way today.

HISTORIC IMPACT DEVICES

The short billy club was the traditional truncheon for police officers. It is best suited for an overhand swing onto a person's head. Its range is generally too short for the techniques taught today.

The blackjack is a lump of lead on a springy handle covered with braided leather. Its flexibility allows for a snapping action that increases the momentum of a blow. It's designed to deliver a knockout blow to someone's head that could have dire consequences.

The sap, or slapper, is a lump of lead between two layers of leather. It's more rigid than a blackjack and, theoretically, less likely to crush a skull. It's effectiveness is in striking bone, such as ankles, shins, or wrists. It's handy for close-in fighting. Saps are still manufactured and sold, and police officers still carry them today, but it is a weapon that may look excessive to a judge.

Sap gloves are for sale in some localities, but have been banned in others. This is a leather glove with a pad of powdered lead over the knuckles. Frankly, the best use for sap gloves is to protect your hands when using a two-hand riot baton. The public is likely to put them in a category with brass knuckles—a thug's weapon, not a security officer's.

Palm saps have a similar problem. This is a leather covered pad of lead that covers your palm, with a strap around the back of your hand. A slap in the face with one feels like a hammer blow.

I classify all these devices as "historical," because that is where they belong—in history. They are bound to be construed as weapons of aggression, even if used defensively. None of these devices are viewed as defensive and most cause severe bleeding wounds that require stitches. On the other hand, the baton is backed with a training program which includes a variety of techniques for controlling a subject such as blocking an attack or hitting in places you can't reach with a sap. The baton is designed to be suitable for many things, but it is not a club.

The object of nonlethal force is to gain compliance and control a combative subject, not to knock someone senseless.

STRAIGHT BATON

Here is a quick review of straight baton techniques from Roland Ouellette of R.E.B. Security Training:

A right-handed officer wears the baton on the left, like a sword. With your left hand on the grip, you can punch the baton straight ahead into an aggressor's abdomen. Or you can draw it with your right hand like a sword to intimidate someone. You can be more subtle by putting your right hand behind your back, using the left hand to lift the baton and push the grip back to your hand.

For an effective and versatile baton-carrying technique, lift your hand and clasp the baton horizontally under your upper arm, like a riding crop. While it is more visible, this ready position isn't a threatening presentation and you can deliver a devastating blow.

The following is an exercise to develop one technique of baton movement. Have your partner hang his or her stick about three feet in front of you. Slowly, flip your stick forward as you extend your hand, but be careful that you hit your partner's stick rather than the hand. Retract your stick after the blow is struck. Speed up the action each time you try this. Get a real flipping motion. The tip of your baton travels a lot faster than your hand. With practice, you might even knock the stick out of your partner's hand.

From the hidden-carry position, the baton is ready to block an aggressor's punch, parry a swinging pipe, or stop a kick to the groin.

If an assailant punches at you, simply bring your hand up, with the baton against what is now the outside of your forearm. This provides a hard surface for a fist to strike. If someone swings a piece of pipe with their right hand while your baton is in your right hand, bring it across in front of you, pushing your left hand at the tip of the baton. Your baton is now at a forty-five-degree angle with the grip farther forward than the tip. A bludgeon will glance down your baton and may swing into the assailant's own shin. Keep your lower left hand open to protect your fingers.

To defend against a kick aimed between your legs, flip the tip of the baton to your other hand and extend your arms. The attacker's shin meets the stick before a toe touches your genital area.

You can move a person back by holding the baton as though it were a pool cue, jabbing it through your left hand into the abdomen. Retract it quickly, however, to keep the assailant from grabbing it.

Use the baton to effect pain compliance. An arm lock is more effective if you put the baton under the subject's wrist and over the upper arm. As you raise the grip, you can increase pain.

There is much more to baton technique than these few examples. You will not become adept at any of these techniques without practicing under the supervision of a qualified instructor. And never hit a person in the head with any kind of impact weapon unless it's a situation where you're justified in using deadly force. Remember, a chop to the collarbone can result in death if the collarbone splinters and punctures the trachea or larynx.

SIDE-HANDLE BATON

The baton with a handle on the side was developed in 1971 by Lon Anderson. It is everything a straight baton is, and more.

Ready position with the side handle baton requires that your strong hand grip the side handle, with your other hand wrapped around the short end of the baton, palm side down. The baton extends back under your forearm. Standing in a modified T-stance, left foot forward, you're ready for anything. You can jab the short end into a person's abdomen. Any block performed with a straight baton can be performed with the side-handle baton, and your hand is out of the way. The flipping strike is devastating when you spin the baton using the handle as a pivot.

The side-handle offers more leverage than a straight baton. Baton come-along holds are easier with the side-handle, providing an extra dimension—like a shepherd's crook. It is so effective that Massad Ayoob, director of the Lethal Force Institute, says, "It is unwise to hold this instrument in other than the ready position, since the handle gives so much leverage that whoever is holding it pretty much has control of the weapon."

Using the side-handle baton is so different from a straight baton that specific training and certification is recommended before an officer is allowed to carry it.

EXPANDABLE BATON

Batons are an acceptable and effective tool for the security officer. However, for the plainclothes officer, it isn't easy to conceal a 26-inch stick under a jacket. Dr. Kevin Parsons, president of Armament Systems and Procedures (ASP), recognized this need. James Rohan, then an instructor at the Federal Law Enforcement Training Center in Georgia, had experimented with expandable martial arts tools, but none fulfilled his criteria for police service. The two met at a defensive tactics seminar and, together, developed an expandable baton now called the ASP Tactical Baton. Casco's CAS, Monadnock's Expandable Baton, and the PPCT Tactical Baton are others on the market.

The expandable baton has the advantage of appearing less intimidating than a long stick hanging from a ring on your belt. When collapsed, it is functional for using short stick techniques. For an extended strike, a flip of the wrist extends the baton, even as you swing.

For an overhand or backhand swing, snap your wrist so the baton extends to the front. Try to avoid the outward swings to open the baton, however, as they leave the baton out of action until you swing it back. They are handy if an aggressor is standing toward your strong side.

Once opened, the expandable baton locks open. It's designed to be rigid against a soft surface like a body. You can jab as you would with a straight baton. To close it, kneel and slam the tip on a hard surface.

Lieutenant Rohan runs the Containment and Emergency Response Team of the U.S. Capitol police, and he is commander of the Recruit and Advanced Training Section of the Training Division. Although he intended to develop a concealable baton for plainclothes officers, there are advantages for uniformed officers as well. A police department in my area adopted the ASP as a primary baton.

TARGETS AND NON-TARGETS

There are vulnerable parts of the body that must not be struck with any impact weapon. The head and neck are always off limits. Avoid the solar plexus, where a hard strike could cause internal injuries. Kidneys and the groin are highly sensitive areas that should not be struck with a hard object. Avoid the spine. From the neck to the tailbone, a concentrated blow to the backbone with a baton could cause permanent injury. Avoid striking joints such as elbows and knees with the baton.

There is less likelihood of damage and a high probability for effect if you strike motor points. Medical research has identified many areas of the body where nerves are clustered under a thin layer of muscle and over bone. There are motor points at the top of the calf, on the upper forearm, inside the forearm, and in about a four-inch circle on the inside and outside of the thigh. Striking these areas with your fist, flashlight, or baton causes a temporary motor dysfunction (like hitting your funny bone) that incapacitates a subject for a few seconds. This offers an opportunity to immobilize a subject with handcuffs.

If targeting motor points fails to subdue a subject, aim for the traditional joints. You can explain to the judge that you tried to subdue the subject humanely before you struck a knee or other sensitive area, which is the next step on the force continuum.

PROPER USE OF THE FLASHLIGHT

Consider this scenario: A motorist pulled his car over to the curb when the siren from a police car signaled him to stop. According to testimony, the motorist resisted, scuffled with the two officers who had stopped him, and, consequently, was subdued with their flashlights. The subject later died.

Obviously, beating someone about the head is not a proper use of the flashlight. But, if the flashlight is in your hand, at some point it is likely to be used as an impact weapon.

A TOUCHY SUBJECT

The flashlight in police service is becoming a contradiction; it is a necessary piece of equipment that is falling into such legal disfavor that some police chiefs have prohibited the long, aluminum-body lights. They've also eliminated any training in the proper use of a flashlight. Their theory is that if their officers use only simple flashlights and aren't trained in their proper use, they avoid liability should the flashlight be used to inflict injury.

A light source is a necessity. If you are holding a flashlight when attacked, are you going to drop your only light source to grab your baton? Of course not. You'll use the plastic two-cell or whatever else is at hand to strike the attacker and buy time until you grab a better weapon.

When employed as a defensive device, the flashlight is nothing more than a short baton or a big Kubotan. Flashlight techniques are essentially the same as baton or short stick techniques. Misuse any of these devices and you may be liable for using excessive force. It's well-established that lack of training can incur liability. If officers are issued a proper flashlight and are trained in its defensive use, the department can show a positive liability defense.

FLASHLIGHT HOLDS

Officers hold a flashlight backwards for two reasons: (1) They want to look down the flashlight beam, as when looking into a stopped car or dark basement niches, and (2) they want the light to be "cocked" and ready for defensive use. So the officer holds the light backward with the weak hand, palm up, so the barrel of the light rests on the shoulder as the beam is aimed through the car window.

RETENTION TECHNIQUES

The security officer needs to learn retention techniques for the long-barrel flashlight. Consider a security officer holding a flashlight in the police hold. The officer gestures, pointing the end cap toward the subject who grabs it with his right hand, toward the tail end of the barrel. There are several possible responses.

Grab the light with both hands, then rotate the light in a small clockwise motion. The subject's wrist will bend as the tail of the light points upward. Continue the circular motion until the person's hand is palm up. Forcibly push the tail end of the light down against the subject's wrist, prying the light from under the thumb.

Or you can grab the tail end with your other hand and spin the flashlight like a propeller through the weak point of the subject's grip at the thumb. Or you can grab the tail end with your other hand and, as you step forward with your weak side foot, flip the head of the light down into the subject's groin or stomach.

If the subject has grabbed the tail end, grab the barrel of the light with your other hand, palm down, so both hands are holding it the same way. Slide your leading hand forward and cover the subject's thumb, then force it into the light. This should cause him enough pain to release the grip. Keep your grip and forcibly point the light downward as you step back, bringing the subject to the ground. Keep the arm straight by pulling upward on the light. To prepare for cuffing, walk toward the subject's feet as you keep pulling up on the light. When prone, bend the subject's arm at the elbow and kneel on his shoulder, as you maintain the thumblock and apply the handcuffs.

CAUTION

There are many variations of the techniques you can apply with the flashlight (or baton). While most instructors concentrate training on a few techniques that are easy to remember and natural to execute, most officers don't get a chance to practice what they learn in the often too-brief training classes. An officer needs techniques that will be recalled naturally, without concentration when needed on the job.

Use caution and judgement when applying any defensive technique—there's a fine line between pain compliance and a broken bone. Do not attempt to learn these techniques from a book without receiving training from a qualified instructor.

Chapter 15

HANDCUFFING

If handcuffs are part of the security officer's issued equipment, the record must state that the officer was trained in their proper use. Improper use that leads to an injury could expose the officer and employer to a liability suit.

It should be the employer's policy that detained subjects be handcuffed. This restrains the offender and reduces the opportunity to fight. Remember, once you handcuff someone you become responsible for their safety. They become defenseless, theoretically.

For a technical evaluation of handcuffs, a consumer product list and the metallic handcuff testing report is available from the National Institute of Justice's Technical Assessment Program Information Center (call 800-24-TAPIC; except in Maryland and metropolitan Washington D.C., call 301-251-5060).

MODERN TYPES

The two principal types of handcuffs made today are chain-linked and stiff-hinged. Smith & Wesson offers a line of traditional chain link handcuffs that comply with NIJ standards. Peerless produces a stiff-hinged model, connected with two bicycle-chain-type links. They fold to fit into a handcuff case, but they don't twist. Hiatts of England offers a Tri-Hinge model that is rigid yet folds flat to fit a standard handcuff case. Both the Peerless and Hiatts stiff-hinged cuffs allow for a more expedient method of handcuffing a suspect.

Handcuffs have four principal parts: the swinging arm, the fixed arm, the locking mechanism and ratchet, and the chain or hinge. The traditional handcuff with a chain is the easiest to escape from. It can be broken by persons with some strength, a high tolerance for pain, and some know-how.

Handcuffs of traditional design may be defeated by inserting a narrow piece of metal as a shim (the metal bristles that fall off of street-sweeper brushes are a favorite) into the slot on the locking mechanism where the swinging arm enters it. This forces down the pawls that hold the swinging arm in place. Double locking (explained in this chapter) the cuff prevents this in some models, but is ineffective in others.

Most handcuff keys are universal in design. Be aware that a subject may be concealing a homemade or real handcuff key. Watch for a ballpoint pen that has a key in place of the push button on the top or a small piece of metal attached to the end of the refill. Despite the manufacturer's claims, no handcuff is completely escape-proof.

An advantage of the hinged cuff is that it provides better security against lock picking, and against a prisoner bringing

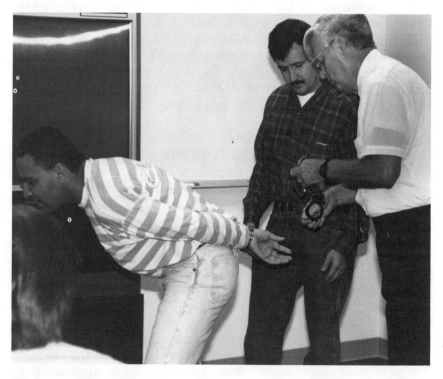

Every security officer has a favorite technique for handcuffing a suspect.

the cuffs from back to front by forcing them under the rump and feet. Rigid-hinge cuffs offer a simple and speedy cuffing technique. With the subject under control and the cuffs in your hand with moving parts down, push the cuffs down. Both cuffs engage respective wrists at the same time.

Plastic handcuffs are popular, especially where multiple demonstrators must be restrained. One style is a single loop that, once tightened around both wrists, does not come open. You have to cut it off. Another style has the locking mechanism in the middle. Each end loops back so you have a cuff on each wrist.

CARRY METHODS

Too often I've seen officers wear a handcuff case right in the small of their back. That puts a chunk of steel right over the spine. A solid punch on the case could cripple you for life. Since cuffs are applied with the strong hand, wear the case on the strong side rear.

MAINTENANCE

Handcuffs seldom require maintenance, but they work better once they are broken in. The action of handcuffs is likely to be rough when new. Simply ratcheting the cuffs through a few hundred times is usually enough to wear away the burrs. You can also use some powdered graphite to lubricate the teeth and hinge. But don't apply too much as it will rub off every time you use the cuffs. Liquid lubricants should be avoided for the same reason.

HANDCUFFING TECHNIQUES

Everyone has a favorite technique for handcuffing a suspect. What is best in a situation depends on the degree of cooperation of the suspect. Remember, there are three times when officers are vulnerable while handcuffing a suspect: (1) when they get into an unsafe position, (2) when they don't have the subject under control, or (3) when they relax too soon.

ALWAYS DOUBLE LOCK THE CUFFS

You can help prevent both escapes and lawsuits by developing the habit of double locking the cuffs whenever you apply them. Double locking prevents movement in either direction. If a prisoner sits on the cuffs and ratchets them down on his or her wrists, pain and injury can result. You may be held liable. The prisoner is likely to say that you put the cuffs on too tightly out of negligence or malice. Adjust the cuffs around the wrist just tightly enough to prevent escape. Be careful with very small people, particularly women with tiny wrists. Push the small pin into the double locking pin hole or slide it in the slot, depending on the brand of cuff you carry.

When removing the cuffs, the key must be turned in both directions to release first the double lock, then the locking pawls.

PROPER SEARCH AND CUFFING
OF AN ARMED SUSPECT

Here is a search and handcuff scenario: A suspect is reported who fits the description of a male armed robber. Don't take any chances. Because the suspect is considered armed and dangerous you must get him into a controllable situation immediately. If you are armed, you're justified in covering him with your gun. Now, how do you approach in order to handcuff the suspect?

A popular technique that is effective and reasonably safe was developed by Robert Downey and Jordan Roth of the California Specialized Training Institute. If the suspect stops after your command of "Security, don't move," tell him, "Raise your hands high." Immediately assume an alert position at a safe distance. Keep him facing away from you. Making him "stretch for the sky" will lift his clothing to reveal weapons tucked into his belt. Even a concealed gun under the tightened shirt should bulge. Order him to turn a full circle slowly, so you get a good look all around.

Then command him to lay spread eagle on the ground with his face away from the direction you plan to approach. Replace your gun into its holster before you approach. Then place a knee into his shoulder and immediately apply a wrist lock. Once you have control, you can cuff his wrists behind his back.

Command him to put his right hand to his back and cuff it, then cuff the left hand—maintaining the wristlock to keep control. Then stand him up for a proper frisk.

If you find the gun he was reported to have, don't stuff it in the front of your pants. There's not only the potential for an embarrassing accident—it also places the gun within the suspect's reach. If you have a backup, hand the gun to the other officer. At least put it behind you once you are sure it is safe. "Never struggle," says Bob Lindsey, former captain with the Jefferson Parish, Louisiana, sheriff's department. "If he resists and you've lost your control hold, create distance for your own sake, and start over."

CUFFING AN UNARMED SUSPECT

In this case, the suspect has "reached for the sky" and turned slowly. You have spotted no weapon, but the ground is muddy so you decide to cuff him standing up.

A popular technique is to command him to spread his feet slightly and put his left hand behind his back and his right hand behind his neck (mirror image for left-handed officers). Now you can reholster your gun while you approach—from a different direction than the suspect last saw you. But be alert. If he flinches, create distance as you draw your weapon. Get a wristlock, a pain-compliance hold, on the arm behind his back. Now you can control him while your right hand cuffs his right wrist up behind his neck. Keeping control, you bring his right hand behind his back and cuff his left wrist. Then walk him to the car while maintaining the wrist or finger lock.

THE WALL IS OUTDATED

Captain George Armbruster of the sheriff's department of Lafayette Parish, Louisiana, has researched handcuffing techniques extensively. He agrees that the technique developed by Downey and Roth is far superior to the old "assume the position against the wall" approach.

When the subject is leaning against the wall, you don't have him in a control hold. So you hook your left foot around his. He can kick you off balance as easily as you can trip him to the ground. Or the subject can push off from the stationary object and attempt to take your gun before you have a chance to draw.

Chapter 16

PATROL

Patrol is a basic function in protecting life, property, and serving the company's interests. Security officers may be responsible for patrolling an office building, a manufacturing complex, or an unincorporated community. There are many kinds of patrol work, from a foot beat to driving a patrol car.

While patrolling inside a building or in a complex, move quietly and don't advertise your presence. If night lights are the only illumination, favor the dark areas. Pause periodically to listen. Note fire or safety hazards.

In one instance, a security officer in a downtown high rise covered her patrol area diligently. One night, she found a major water leak on an upper floor. The damage amounted to $1 million. The company estimates that had she not found the leak early, damage would have exceeded $100 million.

The effectiveness of patrol depends on training and it depends on the officer's attitude. If patrol is considered something to do to pass eight hours, it can be a monotonous chore. If the officer is conscientious, patrol can be interesting. Every area of patrol has its own personality and problems. If an effort is made to know the people, analyze the area, and identify and try to solve problems, the shift will pass quickly. You will feel good about the job.

Patrol is not always pleasant. In fact, the word comes from the French patrouiller, meaning "to go through puddles." That's basically what the officer on patrol does: walks through littered alleys, up rickety back stairs, sloshes through slush in winter and mud puddles in summer.

No officer knows a beat better than the officer on foot. Walking the beat offers the opportunity to chat with people who work in the area, to learn their habits and concerns. Move slowly enough to observe and to detect when something is out of

Proactive patrol involves wearing a distinctive uniform and driving a patrol vehicle with a distinctive color scheme on the light bar.

the ordinary. There are areas you can't observe while sitting in a car. Park it. Turn on your portable radio, put the stick on your belt, and hoof it into the walkway or onto the loading dock to check windows and doors. Walking the beat can still be considered the foundation of effective urban policing.

CONCEPTS OF PATROL

There are many patrol strategies because no single plan works in all places at all times. There are two distinct philosophies of patrol work: proactive and reactive. You may employ both at different times, depending on the situation.

Proactive patrol involves wearing a distinctive uniform and driving a car with a distinctive color scheme and a light bar with flashing emergency lights. The light bar has low-power "glow" bulbs on each side, the "cruise" lights, so it is dimly illuminated at night. On foot, walk on the curb side of the sidewalk. The idea is to be as conspicuous as possible. This technique may be the choice when your purpose is to prevent crime or disturbance.

Proactive patrol is the usual purpose of security. If you are observant, curious, and appear to be everywhere at once, you will:
- Prevent more crime.
- Detect more fires, water damage, intruders, thieves, vandals, and other dangers.
- Help more people.
- Be professional because you're doing a thorough job.

While the officer may be in uniform, reactive patrol involves an unmarked car with emergency lights concealed on the dashboard and rear window shelf. On foot, walk next to buildings, ducking into doorways where you can see without being easily seen. When the purpose of the patrol is apprehension, be unobtrusive. Allow a perpetrator to make the first move. Reactive patrol is the choice when there is a need to observe without influencing a situation or the actions of individuals.

AVOID OBVIOUS ROUTINE

Humans are creatures of habit. For example, you have analyzed your patrol area and determined a patrol routine that covers it effectively and efficiently.

Criminals will learn your routine and plan their actions accordingly. Perhaps it's known that once you check the back door of the drugstore, you won't be back for at least an hour. That gives the criminal time to make an entry.

A smart supervisor once told me, "Be systematically unsystematic. You want people to know you're on the job, but you never want them to know where you'll be next."

HELPFUL TECHNIQUES

Backtracking is just one technique to break a routine, and it works on foot or on wheels. After you have walked a particularly vulnerable area, turn around and walk it back the other way. On your walk back, duck into a doorway and wait for a while.

A university security officer checks the locks on students' bikes.

Observe without being observed. On motor patrol, drive around the block and cover it again, this time cutting up the alley.

When walking a beat at night don't stroll down the street, trying every door, and flashing your light around at random. Even an inexperienced crook can keep track of your movements.

Use light and shadow to your advantage. When entering a dark area from a lighted corridor, wait several minutes while your eyes adjust. This pause also allows you to watch for movement of someone who saw you enter the area. Stand where you are shielded from view so you aren't silhouetted against the lights. Work your way through the dark area by hugging the sides and ducking behind whatever shields you. Use your flashlight only if necessary.

KNOW YOUR AREA

To effectively patrol an area, you must know more than just street names and building numbers. Know the peculiarities of every street, road or alley. For instance, if you follow a car into a street that you know is closed because of road construction, you have an advantage.

Consider the following situation: You're chasing a female subject on foot and she ducks into a building. Where will she go in that building? If you know there's an unlocked door to the basement, but a locked inside door to the interior, you can guess where she is located.

When responding to an armed robbery at a mall store, is there an escape route out the back? Does the proprietor have a barred steel door that is not opened unless a delivery is being made? It would help you to know this in advance. Does a particular real estate office collect rents at the beginning of the month and stash the cash in an old safe? Such knowledge might influence the way you patrol at the beginning of the month.

Which businesses in the mall are similar to those being burglarized in other areas? Where do they keep valuable inventory or large amounts of money? What are the most vulnerable potential points of entry? Is the business equipped with an alarm system? If so, what kind? Does the system sense perimeter intrusion or is it a pressure pad at a vulnerable area inside? And where is the safe, jewelry box, or narcotics cabinet? At night, is there supposed to be a light on in the back of the store? Is that revolving yellow light outside a warning of a burglary or does it indicate that power to the freezer is off?

In most security situations, a primary concern is fire and fire hazards. Know the location of all fire safety equipment and check daily to make sure it is present and accessible. Employees will thoughtlessly block access to fire doors and lanes, fire extinguishers and sprinklers. Are exit lights lit? Be alert. Your nose will tell you about oily rags stashed in a corner and other fire hazards. Buildings and factories have electric motors that run continuously. Watch and smell for overheated bearings. Don't smoke while on patrol. With a cigarette burning under your nose, you won't smell a fire.

Safety hazards are more likely to be discovered by the security officer than any other employee. You are the trained

After hours, "rattling" door handles is a necessary chore.

observer. Finding a cause of a potential accident before it happens may save your company a lot of time and money. Examples include unlocked doors that should be locked, slippery floors, poorly lighted stairs, burned out lights, potholes, broken locks, doors that stick, sharp edges on equipment and chains or pipes hanging dangerously low.

KNOW YOUR PEOPLE

Unauthorized persons are a security officer's concern. Practice monitoring employee ID badges. Although you will recognize most employees personally—check their ID. An employee may have recently lost a job and is returning to the workplace seeking revenge.

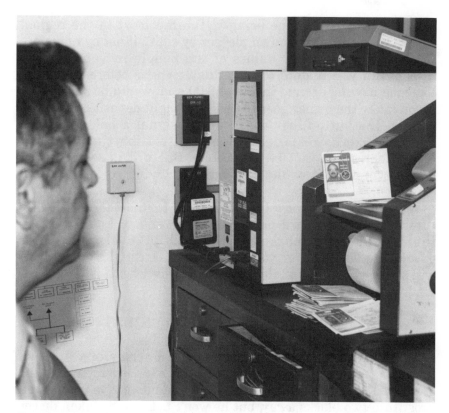

Issuing employee ID badges is often the responsibility of security.

You can't do a good job of patrol unless you know the people and have earned their confidence and respect. Your professionalism and public relations skills reinforce your performance as a security officer.

Cultivate the friendship of the many people whose jobs put them in a position to help you. Delivery persons or any others who cover a daily route around your premises can be a second set of eyes.

Even before computers became common, many mall security departments kept a card file on each business in the mall with names, phone numbers, locations of possible entry, and sensitive points. Use the same idea on your beat. Every patrol area has locations where trouble is likely to develop. Identify those areas that have had the most calls for service, that have been held up before, or that fit a type being victimized most in the region. Know the proprietors and employees by sight, if not by name.

Learn the personal habits of the people in your area of responsibility. If a store manager never opens before 9:00 a.m., someone moving around inside at 8:00 a.m. would be suspicious. If you know the owner goes to the bank night deposit box at 4:00 p.m. on the button, her absence may signal a holdup. If you know the clerks restock shelves after closing time, activity inside then might not be suspicious. But if it is someone you don't recognize, it could be a burglar trying to look like an employee.

While getting to know the people, get to know their vehicles. After a few weeks in a patrol area, you should know the cars that are normally parked in the back lot overnight. After developing this feel for your patrol area, a car that doesn't fit will strike you as out of place and worth investigating.

IMPROVE OBSERVATION SKILLS

It's human nature to see an area in terms of your own interests. A sign painter sees the signs; a salesperson sees the stores that sell her product. The vice squad detective may spot a prostitute two blocks away, but he won't notice a drunken driver unless the driver causes an accident. Learn to observe people, to note their differences and distinguishing features. Practice glancing at people quickly, then describing them. Working strictly from your description, could another officer pick an individual from a crowd?

Some officers appear to have a sixth sense that tells them "that person is wrong." These officers have simply learned to observe details of dress, actions, mannerisms, and appearance that suggest something is out of place. These details may be so minor as to seem meaningless until viewed in context of the total picture.

Look for the differences—such as unusual acts or manner of dress. Someone paying inordinate attention to you might bear watching. One who seems indifferent to you may be trying to hide nervousness.

There are certain areas where people normally congregate. You can expect to find kids in front of the theater when the last show lets out, especially if there's an ice cream store next door. What if the stores are closed and a suspicious male is hanging around? Position yourself so you can observe without being obvious. What's he looking at? Did he take notice of you as you passed? It could be he's the lookout for his partner who is jimmying the narcotics locker in the drugstore. If you do approach and question him, look for signs of nervousness, frequent glances in a particular direction. He may try to divert your attention or encourage you to run him in. That's a good time to check doors and windows. Look for marks on door jams or scratches on locks.

Most people around transportation terminals carry luggage. Does the quality of luggage fit the dress of the person carrying it? Are travelers being approached by people they don't seem to know? Look for youngsters who appear unfamiliar with the town and appear to have no destination. Does the person fit the profile of a drug courier or fugitive?

Every time you make a successful detention, ask yourself, "What tipped me off that something was wrong? What attracted my attention?" By analyzing each situation you will discover the apparently insignificant action or detail that didn't fit. If you have a partner, talk it over. You'll find that the vague feeling you get when "something is wrong" has sound basis from your observations.

USING THE SPOTLIGHT

You seldom see a passenger car equipped with a spotlight unless it's a patrol car. Driving through dark alleys, flashing the spotlight around, is a sure tipoff to the criminal. Use the spotlight the same as you do your flashlight when you're on foot—sparingly.

Become familiar with your spotlight. Practice pointing it at the spot you want to illuminate. Turn it on for just a second and turn it right off. If you need to move the beam from one side of the street to the other, turn it off as the light points down the street. Shining a spotlight down the block will warn a perpetrator many blocks away.

SITUATIONS THAT CALL FOR CAUTION

Fools rush in where angels fear to tread. When you check the exterior of a building and find evidence of forced entry, or smoke, call for backup or the fire department.

For example, while on patrol you spot a car that doesn't belong in the area where it's parked. You radio the dispatcher who checks with police and they report the car stolen. Do you rush over and start rummaging through it for evidence? Of course not. Better to position yourself where you can watch it discretely, particularly if it was recently stolen. The thief may return to the vehicle. Advise the dispatcher what you have observed. Perhaps a plainclothes police officer will want to stake it out. Once you're reasonably sure the car has been abandoned, you might feel the hood to see if it's warm. Look for shiny scratches, signs of recent damage. Check the interior (through the windows, don't touch the doors) for visible contraband. Look to see if the ignition switch has been popped. But let police investigators do the searching. They're trained to find evidence not obvious to you.

If responding to an armed robbery call, you may find the perpetrator still in the store with sales clerks and customers. Rushing in could be dangerous to someone inside, or even create a hostage situation. Better to wait a discreet distance away for the suspects to come out before confronting them.

Narcotics cases can be touchy. The local police narcotics squad may work a case for months without making an arrest. Many people are involved in the drug business, with one level shielding the next higher group. If you rush in and bust the dealer, you could blow the case of a police officer who was using the dealer to identify his distributor. If you come across a drug transaction and can discreetly check by radio, do it—get the expert's advice first.

DOGS IN SECURITY SERVICE

A security K-9 unit is an officer and dog team who work patrol and support others. This may involve searching a building for an intruder or looking for contraband. An officer with a dog provides capabilities far beyond an officer alone.

Robert S. Eden, a constable with the Delta, British Columbia, Canada, police department, has trained dogs professionally and privately. One of his experiences shows how the team could virtually see in the dark

Eden was working a stakeout at a drug drop in an open area on a dark, moonless night with a suspect who was wise to the possibility of surveillance. It was not possible to use additional officers to cover the area—only Eden and his dog were in position. "Suddenly, my dog lifted his head, ears intently forward. Obviously, someone I couldn't see was walking across the site," Eden explains. "The dog's head slowly panned left to right as he focused on the suspect's movements. At this point, backup was called and the apprehension was successfully concluded."

DOG'S SPECIAL TALENTS

The dog is a loving companion who seeks your approval. A K-9 dog is not a vicious guard or attack dog, but a working "security officer" who is caring and protective until circumstances require aggression. A dog has unique talents.

It's a common misconception that dogs have poor eyesight. Tests have shown they can focus clearly on objects more than 100 yards away. And as Eden's nighttime example shows, dogs have far better night vision than humans. A dogs' keen sense of smell and ability to identify scents specific to an individual are demonstrated by tracking dogs. And dogs hear a higher range of frequencies than humans. Some say the dog has six times the hearing capacity of humans.

K-9 assignments are not for everyone. You're always on call. You may be relegated to the less desirable shifts. Officers working K-9, however, wouldn't have it any other way. There is a personal satisfaction when the team of officer and dog can accomplish tasks no one else in your group can. And you couldn't have a more devoted partner.

Chapter 17
Pitfalls of Patrol

There are many hazards and dangers inherent to patrol work, besides the problems of boredom, indifference, and fatigue.

FOOT PATROL

Bob Matteucci of the North Wildwood, New Jersey police department cautions security officers to be identifiable. "Down here at the Shore resorts, we have seasonal security guarding the amusement piers after hours during the summer months. Problem is that the people working are almost always not in uniform nor do they wear any sort of identification. On one occasion, while investigating a trespass call at an amusement pier, a man walked up to me with a stick, yelling. Luckily, my partner recognized him as a security officer from the adjacent pier, or things could have turned ugly. He was trying to point out where he had last seen the trespassers."

If you lack two-way radios and patrol an area without phones, one solution might be the use of a cordless phone. An amusement area hired its own security officers to make rounds during the night. They had no radio system or dispatcher. When the officers saw something suspicious, they had to run back to the office to make a phone call. One officer brought a cordless phone to work and tied it into the phone system. Now, while making rounds, he has direct communication to the police. He can call in from his observation site and provide updates. Many businesses have a cordless phone. Ask them to leave it out for you.

Portable cellular phones are another option for the lonely security officer without a two-way radio. The point is that communication is critical. If no one has thought of how you're going to communicate, think of a way yourself.

MOBILE PATROL

If an accident happens in the northbound lanes, the southbound traffic will tie up with onlookers. Security officers are people, too, and perhaps even more curious than passersby. Don't respond to an emergency call unless you are dispatched to it. The assigned officer doesn't need a pack of patrol cars causing congestion and possibly blocking an ambulance or fire truck.

When you are dispatched on an emergency call, remember that your first job is to reach your destination safely. Drive carefully, don't cause an additional traffic accident by a too rapid response.

DEFENSIVE DRIVING

The largest single source of liability suits is due to automobiles, not to firearms or the use of force. Your car is a very powerful tool, and you use it constantly. If your job entails patrol, operating your car demands exemplary skills behind the wheel. A marked car is easily identifiable and the world is watching.

Some of the skills taught in a defensive driving course include control, steering, fast but safe lane changes, U-turns, control of skids, and proper braking.

Driving instructors know the causes of officer-involved accidents and have developed techniques to help you avoid them. They will also try to teach you judgment. Their experience will tell you what you might expect from other drivers' reacting to you. That is the essence of defensive driving—anticipating other drivers' actions

Draping an arm out the window while resting the right hand at the bottom of the wheel may seem comfortable, but it affords little steering control. Where does the racing driver put his hands? The left is placed at nine or ten o'clock, the right at three or two o'clock. This is the hand position that provides optimum control.

Brake as you enter a tight turn, slowly accelerate during the turn. Too much braking or acceleration during a turn could cause fishtailing or a skid.

If a suspect is traveling in the other direction, several types of U-turns can be made to reverse direction quickly. The simple "U" is the quickest and safest when you have room. When you don't, you can back into a drive on the right side or turn into a left-side road, then back into the street. The Y-turn is a last resort. It involves turning your nose to the right, then backing in a left turn across the road so you're nearly headed in the other direction. If traffic is heavy, it's dangerous.

Intersections are a problem. New York City loses about 400 police cars a year in intersection crashes, according to local news media. Many involve two cruisers with lights and sirens blaring. Although other drivers are supposed to give way to your lights and siren, they often don't. If you enter an intersection at 90 mph, the other driver will never see you until you collide. You are responsible. Brake enough to avoid crossing traffic, then accelerate after clearing the intersection

A security force in an unincorporated community may have police-like patrol duties. Many police departments now prohibit high speed chases. When the security officer does choose pursuit, the purpose of lights and siren is to clear a path so you can reach your destination safely. Remember, you don't want a parade following one lonely suspect. You can position other cars ahead as long as one officer handles the pursuit. If the suspect takes off at high speed, you have the suspect vehicle's description and plate number. Ask your dispatcher to relay it to police and let them handle it

With a roof-mounted siren wailing and radio blaring, it is noisy inside a car. You must keep the dispatcher informed of your location, speed, and direction of travel, while maintaining a legible transmission. Try using the microphone like a throat mike if the message isn't clearly transmitting. Press it against your neck, on the soft area next to your windpipe. While it blocks the background noise it lets your voice come through your throat with perhaps a 25 percent reduction in audio.

Treat every emergency call like an emergency. "Routine" is a threat to the security officer. The seventh response to a particular alarm that's always false may be real. You can't assume anything. Until you determine the facts, every call is an emergency.

If possible, avoid being observed while approaching the scene of an emergency call. In an urban area, approach on a parallel street and cut over at the last possible intersection. If it's a holdup, burglary, or prowler call, extinguish your vehicle lights before they are observed by the suspects. Note the registration numbers of vehicles or persons departing as you near the scene.

Upon arriving, stop down the street and observe the scene. Is someone waiting in a car with the engine running, or fleeing on foot in the opposite direction? If nothing attracts your attention, identify the best approach route before you move. Have a plan. If you're working with a partner, it's critical that each of you knows what the other is going to do. Talk about it. A poor plan is better than no plan at all.

HAZARDS

The security officer can't avoid hazardous situations, but you can understand them and learn the proper responses.

Electrical Hazards

There is no "safe" level of electrical shock. The shock from 120-volt house current can kill just as easily as a 115,000-volt transmission line.

Security officers may be called upon to respond to an accident in which a car has hit a utility pole and knocked lines down, or a tree limb has fallen causing broken wires. Fallen power lines may flail around and spark, or lie quietly, giving no indication that they are "hot." Stay at least 10 feet from any fallen wire and assume it is live.

The first thing to do on arrival is to call in and ask that the utility be notified. Give the location and, if you can get it safely, the pole number. Set out flares and keep bystanders at least 100 feet away. If it's raining, wet ground increases the hazard. Keep people away from metal fences, highway dividers, or anything else that might conduct electricity outside of your safety perimeter.

Like lightning, electricity will seek the ground. Keep yourself and others from locations between downed lines or between a wire and the ground. When a fallen wire is draped over an automobile, you can assume that the metal shell of the car is hot. If the car is occupied, tell the occupants to stay where they are. As long as they remain inside the vehicle, they won't complete the circuit to the ground. If they must leave the safety of the car's interior, as in the danger of fire, tell them to jump completely free of the car before they hit the ground. Don't touch the car and the ground at the same time.

If a wire has fallen on a victim, don't try to remove it with a tree limb. If the wood is moist, it could conduct electricity. A long, dry rope may be used. Try to move the dangerous part of the wire while leaving other parts in contact with the ground to reduce the danger.

A writhing wire may be stabilized by rolling a spare tire onto it. If possible, wait for the utility crew to arrive with proper equipment.

Hazardous Materials

A tanker truck spill can involve a number of hazardous substances, from gasoline and other chemicals to radiological materials. Each may require a different procedure for handling the spill. When you reach the scene of an accident involving hazardous materials, help is only a radio call away.

The dispatcher should have a copy of the U.S. Department of Transportation's *Hazardous Materials Emergency Response Guidebook* (DOT-P 5800.2). It lists the code numbers posted on the diamond-shaped placard on the exterior of trucks and listed on shipping papers. The code will identify the substance. With each entry is a guide number that refers to an outline of potential hazards to health, fire, or explosion, and recommended remedial actions including type of fire extinguisher, how to handle a spill or leak, and first aid procedures

Explosives and blasting agents are not listed by number, but a guide sheet is provided for Class A, Class B, and Class C explosives. Classes, defined in Department of Transportation regulations, rate explosives by the hazard they represent. Class A can detonate and are a maximum hazard, B are highly flammable, and C includes articles that may contain A or B explosives but in a quantity limited so as to be a minimum hazard.

CHEMTREC, the Chemical Transportation Emergency Center, has a 24-hour 800 number. It is a public service of the Chemical Manufacturers Association in Washington, D.C. They can usually provide hazard information warnings and guidance if you give them the identification number or name of the product and the nature of the problem.

The National Sheriff's Association (NSA) has an information service called HAZMAT that offers hazardous material information through NSA's computer data base, accessible through the National Law Enforcement Telecommunications System. Call in the substance ID number off the placard and the police dispatcher can send a message query addressed to NSA's HAZMAT system and, within seconds, receive appropriate instructions for emergency action.

HAZMAT and CHEMTREC work together to give the first responder a fast identification of the material, define the hazards, and explain the actions to be taken until hazardous materials units can respond. The data base is updated frequently with current information, so it may be more accurate—certainly more up-to-date—than the printed guidebook.

What is the proper initial response? Call in the number off the placard. Keep onlookers safely away from the spill. Stay upwind and out of low areas. Isolate the hazard area and deny entry to everyone except trained HAZMAT units. You may need to wear protective clothing or breathing apparatus. Do not walk into or touch any spilled material. Avoid inhaling any gases, fumes, and smoke even if no hazardous materials are involved. Evacuate any area in the path of a drifting cloud, don't assume it's harmless just because you can't smell it.

REPORTING HAZARDOUS CONDITIONS

As the only company representative who travels the hallways and byways of your area around the clock, you're in the best position to note and report hazards and nuisances. In fact, you may face the prospect of a lawsuit for "failure to protect" if you do nothing.

It's up to you to ask your dispatcher to notify the proper agency in case of streetlight outages, unprotected manholes, or icy spots on the road. It's up to you to remove vehicles parked in hazardous locations, assist stranded motorists, or help a confused elderly person get home. If you allow an intoxicated person to wander the area and that person is hit by a car, you may be liable.

Chapter 18
TRAFFIC CONTROL

If your employer's service covers an unincorporated community or industrial complex, traffic control is likely to be part of the job. Employee parking lots and roads on the company premises are in your jurisdiction. You have no authority on the public highway, even just outside your parking lot entrance, unless there is some arrangement with local police.

Traffic control is important. There are more than 172 million vehicles in the United States and almost four million miles of public roads. Motor vehicles have killed more Americans than all the wars in which the United States participated. Auto accidents are so commonplace that even fatalities may not make the evening news. Yet, witnessing a fatal accident will test the strength of your stomach. While it may seem mundane, effective motor vehicle enforcement can potentially save more lives than anything else you do.

MOTOR VEHICLE LAWS

Traffic laws are much the same in all jurisdictions, but they can differ in detail. There are model traffic laws, such as the Uniform Vehicle Code published by the National Committee on Uniform State Traffic Laws and Ordinances. It's up to you to learn the specific laws that apply to your circumstances.

Traffic codes are intended to promote the safe movement of traffic. Common sense is the basis for traffic laws. Essentially, these laws evolved in response to problems identified by police officers, and they change in response to deficiencies officers discover during their daily routine.

RULES OF THE ROAD

Some vehicle statutes are crimes, particularly auto theft or drunken driving. The security officer's involvement in enhancing public safety and preventing accidents on the employer's premises most often concerns the category of moving violations.

1. Failure to keep to the right. As a rule, all traffic codes require driving to the right and delineate the exceptions: passing to the left, vehicle signaling a left turn, traffic on a one-way street. There are exceptions such as passing on the right a car traveling in the center lane of a three-lane roadway. It is unsafe to cross two lanes in order to pass on the left.
2. Making an improper turn. "Cutting corners," swinging wide unnecessarily, turning right or left from anywhere other than the right-most or left-most lane, and most U-turns are all violations.
3. Failing to obey a traffic signal. Too many impatient drivers think an amber light means "speed up before it turns red." They forget that it really means "prepare to stop." The exception is when directed otherwise by an officer.
4. Failing to obey a stop sign. Stop at a stop sign, obviously, but where exactly? A limit line may be marked. At a marked pedestrian crossing, it's the near-side line for approaching vehicles. If unmarked, it's a line extended from the edge of the crossroad.
5. Failing to obey the signal of an officer. While this law applies to police officers, by implication it puts teeth in the security officer's traffic direction.
6. Failing to signal when stopping or turning. The purpose of these laws is to require drivers to make their intentions known to others. Though some motorists seem to think that signaling gives them some sort of right of way, it does not.
7. Failing to yield right of way. Motor vehicle codes use many words to define all the conditions and circumstances that determine which vehicle has the right of way. If you're involved in traffic enforcement, you will have to learn your state's code. Basically, however, they boil down to common sense.

A campus security officer tickets illegally parked cars.

The vehicle having the right-of-way usually is the one on a thoroughfare, the one on the right, or the one that arrived at the intersection first. When New Hampshire found drivers racing each other to be first at the intersection, they changed the law. Now it's only the one on the right. A favorite question of one of my instructors was, "If a responding ambulance, fire truck, police car, and mail truck arrive at an intersection at the same time, which has the right of way?" Technically, it's the mail truck. Under the U.S. Constitution, nothing can impede the U.S. mail. Practically, however, the mail carrier gives way.

8. Operating a vehicle in a reckless manner. Statutes vary in their definition of "reckless driving." Some are quite broad: "operation of a vehicle on any highway in willful and wanton

Security responsibilities in an industrial complex often include traffic control.

disregard for the safety of persons or property." In Connecticut, a driver who proceeds through a marked crosswalk containing pedestrians is driving recklessly. "Recklessness" is more than mere negligence. It is a failure to perform because of carelessness or oversight, or failure to act in a manner common to a "reasonable and prudent" driver.

9. Speeding. In addition to exceeding posted speed limits, speeding statutes include such phrases as "reasonable speed," "safe speed," and "road conditions." For example, a highway with a posted 55 mph limit could be unsafe at any speed above 40 mph in a snowstorm. Or heavy pedestrian traffic could make driving at the posted speed limit unsafe. Study your state's laws to see just how such statutes are

worded. Driving too slow can also create a hazard and may constitute a violation.

10. Driving while intoxicated. This is another area that differs widely from state to state. The trend among police is to use the roadside check as probable cause for administering a breath, blood, or urine analysis. Anything more than .10 parts per million blood alcohol level is considered too drunk to drive. Some states have an implied consent law. If drivers refuse the test, their license is automatically suspended for a time.

11. Operating a vehicle with defective brakes or other equipment. Brakes, windshield wipers, horn, lights, and tires are all considered safety equipment on a motor vehicle. Enforcing these statutes removes an unsafe vehicle from the road, and it's an action usually requiring correction rather than a court appearance. It also gives you reasonable grounds for a stop which may lead to the discovery of a more serious crime. Many burglars have met their demise because their car had a burned-out tail light.

The conduct of pedestrians is usually covered in the traffic code. Such provisions came into law recently so there is surprising uniformity across the country.

Leaving the scene of an accident is a violation. Evading responsibility, as one state calls it, also carries a social stigma because of the possible consequences. In an accident involving personal injury, the hit-and-run driver may contribute to a death by leaving the victim unattended or without first aid.

A traffic code will require anyone involved in an accident to stop, identify oneself, and render aid. But at what point does leaving become "evading?" Is one who leaves the scene to go call for help an evader? And what if a driver is unaware that an accident has happened? For instance, in one case the rear of a tractor-trailer hit the front of a small car. In another, a passenger exiting the rear door of a bus caught her arm and was dragged. In both cases the operator had no idea anything was wrong.

FRAUDULENT LICENSES

Because they are a popular form of identification when cashing checks or proving one is old enough to order a drink, driver licenses are a prime target for forgery. The laminate of a legitimate license can be split so a birth date can be changed, or a complete fraudulent license can be manufactured.

Providing fraudulent licenses is big business. The New York City Police once assigned several youthful officers to go undercover and infiltrate gangs. The officers claimed they received many speeding tickets and subsequent suspensions, and within two weeks they found four men who trafficked in forged licenses. If there is anything suspicious about the license a motorist hands you, check it carefully.

Persons carrying forged or altered licenses are often chronic offenders whose licenses have been suspended or they are high point violators who may use a forgery to keep their real license clean. Under-age youths who are too young to get a license or who can't afford high insurance premiums also use altered licenses. While holding the operator's license, ask the date of birth and full name and address of the driver. An operator with a forgery may not remember the fictitious address, or may even forget the name.

INTEGRITY OF ENFORCEMENT

Corruption in law enforcement doesn't begin with thousand-dollar bribes. It begins with fixing tickets. That's not to say there aren't circumstances where a ticket shouldn't be revoked. In one situation a town meeting drew some 5,000 citizens to the high school auditorium. The crowd overflowed into the gymnasium where closed-circuit television was set up to show testimony pertinent to a town issue. People were parked all over the area. There was an ordinance against parking on the grass, but the circumstances were unusual. One officer ticketed only those cars parked illegally in handicapped spaces. Another sergeant dispatched a cruiser to ticket the cars on the grass. The chief later rescinded hundreds of tickets issued that night, except the ones for the handicapped parking.

On a college campus or in an unincorporated community, directing traffic can prevent tie-ups and accidents.

DIRECTING TRAFFIC

It is usually not an efficient use of personnel to assign an officer to direct traffic. A traffic signal works 24 hours a day and doesn't need relief to go to the bathroom. But there are circumstances—road construction, an accident, disaster, parade, or other special events—where you must make sure traffic flows as smoothly as possible. There can be a certain satisfaction in suddenly finding yourself the "point man" in officer contact with employees.

You'll be asked every question you can imagine. You are the target of everyone who is confused or lost, and it's amazing how many motorists have no idea where they are. You must be polite, try to avoid sarcasm, and leave everyone thinking nice thoughts about you and your company.

Your job is to expedite the smooth flow of traffic. You have to get crowds of sports spectators across the busy street or empty out the parking lot onto the thoroughfare without congesting normal traffic. Or perhaps your assignment is to keep onlookers away from a disaster scene, yet leave a route for emergency vehicles to enter and exit quickly.

I'll never forget my baptism in traffic direction. I was so young and green I had not yet learned the indifference that plagues veteran officers. It was on old Route 1 between Baltimore and Washington, a four-lane highway with two lanes in each direction, and only a double white line to separate the two. This stretch of highway had been dubbed "Bloody Mary" by the media.

One of a convoy of military trucks carrying ammunition had an accident. The fire chief had closed the road for fear of an explosion. That road couldn't be closed for more than a few seconds without causing a major traffic jam.

A state trooper placed me at the south end and another town officer at the north end of the accident area to close the road. Since I knew the area, I motioned the first car in the right line to approach me. I gave directions to turn right, go two blocks down, turn left two more blocks, then left again to get back onto the highway beyond the accident. I asked the driver to go slow because a line of cars would be following him.

Consider that there were two lines of cars coming at me. So often, one line moves more quickly than the other and drivers try to switch lanes, causing more accidents. I stood just above the turnoff and motioned one car from each line at a time. The drivers soon picked up on the idea they were taking turns, and it worked. Both lines progressed slowly, no one tried to change lanes, and everyone was happy.

GIVING GOOD SIGNALS

Directing traffic is part of basic training, but many officers seem to forget or become lackadaisical. Too many officers are injured each year while directing traffic, so pay attention to these cautions.

Drivers cannot follow your directions if they don't understand your signal. I've seen officers, arm down by their side, meekly wave their hand or flap their fingers, and expect a driver who is 30 feet away to understand their gesture. In my experience, the rigidly formal gesturing taught in military police school is the most understandable.

First, on a traffic post, wear a reflective vest and reflective gloves. The traditional upraised hand to signal "Stop" is barely noticeable if you're wearing black gloves at dusk. It's not only for your own protection, it helps your case when you testify against the driver who ran through your signal. Use decisive arm (not hand) movements. If you wave cars to pass in front of you, wave your hand in front. If they should pass behind you, bring your hand up and behind your head. If you want them to turn left inside of you, move your hand in that direction. If they should turn around you, sweep your hand around.

Stopping a line of traffic is a problem. The cars nearest you may not have time to stop. Wave them through with your left hand held low as you point with your right hand at a car farther back in the line that you want to stop. You must get the driver's attention before you can give a signal, and pointing purposefully at one particular car can be surprisingly effective. Standing on a safety island or between the lanes makes it easier as you play the matador in a bullfight.

In my part of the country you seldom see a brass whistle as part of the uniform any more, but it is a good tool. A long blast on the whistle, coupled with an upturned palm, means "Stop." Two quick blasts, with a wave, means "Start." And a series of three or more short blasts means "Stop Now."

DIRECTING TRAFFIC AFTER DARK

A reflective traffic vest and gloves are important during daylight. At night they're mandatory, but not adequate. Flares set in a pattern to slow and shift oncoming traffic around an accident will be observed by traffic long before traffic sees you. Unless you're standing in the headlight beams—which is a place you don't want to be—drivers may have a hard time seeing reflective garments.

Use a flashlight to extend your signal. People interpret a horizontally waving light as a stop signal. When you point it forward and raise it vertically like a come-on wave, they will move in the indicated direction.

In large expanses where access roads may run straight for miles, your signals need to extend much farther than the isolated flare on a city street. Flares, light sticks, flashlight, flashlight with a red baton, traffic cones, overhead floodlights, a parked cruiser with lights flashing, barricades with flashing yellow lights—use whatever is available to protect yourself while directing traffic.

Chapter 19
PHYSICAL SECURITY

One complaint that public emergency services have with private security is delay in calling in an alarm. Some officers feel they are entirely responsible for handling "situations," and are reluctant to ask for help until the situation has escalated beyond their ability to control it.

This problem is not unique to private security officers. A similar circumstance can occur with airline pilots. Few will call "Mayday" until the situation is hopeless. They seem to feel that, by declaring an emergency, they are admitting that they have lost control of the situation. An airliner that crashed on Long Island for lack of fuel is a good example. The pilot reported low fuel, but did not declare an emergency.

The security officer may also be faced with conflicting orders. Seldom is there a written policy that states "do not call for emergency services." But the officer is made aware that business interruptions, evacuations, and publicity are not wanted by the employer.

Many businesses require that the security officer first determine if the alarm is real before calling an emergency service. This can cause delay. Suppose a smoke alarm is sounding in an air handler located above the ceiling space. First, the air handler location has to be determined from a map or diagram. An officer responds to that location, then finds a ladder to get above the ceiling space to check for fire. Most alarms are false, so a procedure such as this may *appear* to be justified.

There are many documented cases where a delayed alarm to the fire service has caused large losses in dollars and lives. Hotels and office buildings are the most vulnerable to this scenario.

Problems with burglar alarms are similar—you don't want to bother the police with what is probably a false alarm. Sometimes police encourage this attitude by negative comments

Checking alarm systems is the responsiblity of most security departments.

while answering one of numerous false alarms. In one mall, three or so burglary alarms, both silent and audible, going off a week are common. Usually occurring within a half hour of the store closing, these are often caused by bad alarm setting by employees. If they are taken for granted, however, some unarmed security officer may walk in on a burglary in progress.

Charles Fuhrman, owner of Fuhrman Investigations, Inc., of Phoenix, Arizona, says, "My advice is to call for help when you first learn of an incident. It can always be canceled if necessary. Give the information known about the situation and let the emergency service decide on the appropriate response. In the example about the concealed air handler sending a smoke alarm, notify the fire department that you have an alarm, there are no indications of fire, and that you are checking. Let them decide whether to send one engine or a full first alarm assignment."

146

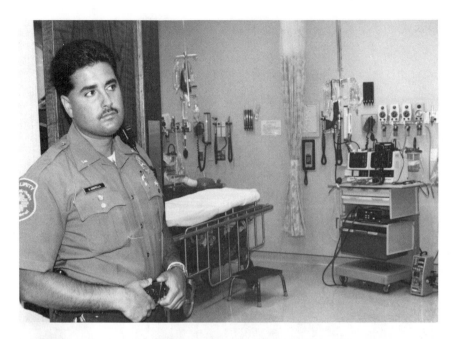

A hospital security officer stands at his post in the emergency room.

ACCESS CONTROL

Controlling access is a concern even in public places. For example, shopping malls are open to the public but have various areas marked "Employees Only." Controlling access in a defense plant is easier because only certain people may enter the facility. Hospitals are open to the public, have varying levels of access authorization, and cannot afford to place a guard at every door.

For example, one hospital with six entrances experienced problems with equipment theft and with strangers sleeping in empty rooms. To control access, all but one entrance was closed and card readers were installed at every secure entrance and interior door. Each employee was issued a photo ID card with an embedded invisible magnetic strip. To go through a locked door, the employee would run the ID card through the reader. A computer compared the individual's authorization with the particular door and, if authorized, the door would unlock. The computer recorded the date and time the employee used that door.

Access control to this building is accomplished with a keypad system requiring a number code to unlock a door.

Another system available maintains a photograph of the individual employee. When the employee uses the card for access, a television camera shows who is at the door. The computer retrieves the employee's photo and puts it on the split screen beside the camera image. The officer can compare the two before unlocking the door.

Newer hotels have gotten away from the old room key idea, with every housekeeper having a master key. The keys are easily copied. One hotel I was in recently issued a metal card with holes in it. A computer programs the lock of my room to work only with that card. If I were to lose the key card, a different combination would be issued and my lost card would no longer open the door.

It's amazing how much faith people put in the simple locks on desk drawers and cabinets. In one instance, an advertising agency was working on a gun manufacturer's account. An executive stored sample guns in an overhead cabinet. When he went to retrieve them the next day, they weren't there. There was no evidence of tampering, and the lock was firmly in place. An officer explained loose tolerances in such modular units and demonstrated by pushing up on the door slightly. It opened with ease and re-closed the same way, leaving no evidence of having ever been opened.

FENCING

Perimeter access control includes the exterior walls of the facility, cliffs, rivers, or, most commonly, fences. The average chain link fence will not stop a determined intruder. A security fence must be at least eight feet high, usually with seven feet of fence with a one-foot top of barbed or razor wire. The advantage of chain link is you can see through it. The most secure chain link has mesh of less than two inches. Otherwise, each is a toehold that makes climbing easy. To prevent digging under fencing, the foot must be set in concrete.

After the security consultant designs the fencing, the landscaper comes along to make it pretty. Often, plots of small bushes are added to enhance the appearance of the area. In a few years those shrubs are big bushes that could hide an assault force. Lighting the fence at night accomplishes little if you provide places to hide.

Fence alarms aid the security officer who can't be everywhere at once. Some use cable that causes a current to flow and activate an alarm if it's flexed. "Electric eyes" and laser beams are also used to detect movement. In very sensitive areas, the perimeter may be a double row of fencing with a dog run between the fences.

Recognizing deficiencies in physical security systems is part of your job as a security officer. Listed here are some of the more common deficiencies. Put yourself in the burglar's place and imagine how you might gain entry. For instance, imagine there is a drainage tunnel leading from a rusty grate by the river outside the fence to a point directly under the cash room. That should be the subject of a deficiency report. Report it in writing so it can be brought to the attention of those responsible. This will show that you're doing your job.

ALARM SYSTEMS

There are many different kinds of alarm systems on the market. A system may include one or a combination of the following:

—A local alarm that simply rings a nearby bell.

—A proprietary alarm that sends a signal to your security control office.

—A central station alarm that notifies the control center of an outside contracted service.

—Or, in rare cases, a direct-connect alarm that activates a signal at the local police station.

In many areas, you may no longer install an alarm system connected directly to the police. Where such connections still exist, some police departments impose a fee for false alarms. This is another reason for the growth of the private security industry.

SENSORS

There are sensors available which will detect almost any problem imaginable. Window glass with metallic strips around the edges is one example. If the glass is broken, breaking the strip, an alarm sounds. A low-voltage current flows constantly and triggers the alarm when it is interrupted.

A window or door can contain a hidden switch that is held either open or closed, depending on the system, as long as the window or door remains undisturbed. Door mats can hide a pressure-sensitive pad.

Photoelectric devices detect light or the absence of light. Infra-red sensors activate when they detect the heat of a human body. Motion detectors are sonar-like devices which detect the movement of objects in a predetermined area. Acoustic detectors "hear" sounds. Sprinkler systems may include a water flow detector to sound an alarm. Smoke detectors are similar to those found in private homes.

From the communications center officers can monitor a
facility with CCTV, communicate with officers by radio,
answer the phone, dispatch a security patrol or fire engine,
and check employee files on computer.

CCTV

Closed-circuit television has become a vital part of many
physical security systems. Parking garages, hallways, access
doors, and other sensitive areas can be monitored by one
security officer at a panel of television screens. One potential
problem with monitoring CCTV systems, however, is fatigue.
Inattention on the part of the security officer may result in
violations being undetected.

To overcome human error, another system is coming into use for situations involving a static scene. The CCTV camera image is fed to a computer that digitizes the picture. It "memorizes" the scene and "watches" some 65,000 bits of information. If the scene monitored by the computer changes, it triggers an alarm so an officer can check for an intruder.

Some systems simply take a picture on video tape every few seconds. The picture of a bank robber shown on the nightly television news is from a videotape.

The workings of security systems, and how they can be defeated, must be closely guarded from unauthorized individuals.

Chapter 20
FIRE

Fires often occur after employees, except for the security officer, have left for the day. Of all possible hazards, fire is the most potentially damaging to a company. Some have not survived a disastrous fire.

With any private security job, fire is a primary concern. Fire hazards are discussed in more detail in the chapter on Patrol. But what are your duties after a fire has started?

The security officer's sequence of actions are represented by the acronym RACE: Rescue, Alarm, Containment, and Extinguish. A small fire can be easy to extinguish if you know how. The proper type of extinguisher must be matched to the fire and you should know where to locate each type of extinguisher.

TYPES OF FIRES AND EXTINGUISHERS

Class A—wood, cloth, paper, trash. Extinguishers marked "A" contain water. Place your finger partially over the nozzle to create a spray to knock down the fire, then release it and let the water stream soak it thoroughly.

Class B—flammable liquids such as gasoline, oil, paint, solvents. Class B extinguishers may use CO_2, foam, halon, or dry chemical powder to smother the fire. Never use water on these fires—it will cause them to spread, rather than extinguish them.

Class C—electrical equipment. Water is also forbidden on electrical fires. Class C extinguishers may use dry chemicals, halon, or CO_2. With a CO_2 extinguisher, aim at the flame so the gas can replace the oxygen the fire is feeding on. With a halon extinguisher, it's better to aim at the near edge of the fire and sweep it toward the back.

Class D—combustible metals such as magnesium and sodium. Type D extinguishers, usually dry powder, are required for these special circumstances.

You may have concerns other than just putting out a beginning fire, however. Suppose the whole staff is in the office? You might tell one employee to pull the fire alarm. Then hand the proper extinguisher to another employee and give verbal instructions. If the situation warrants, tell others to evacuate the building. Fire drills are supposed to teach evacuation routes. Time is critical, and so is accuracy in reporting the fire. If you have to phone the fire department, identify yourself and the number you're calling from, and give the location of the fire and its nature and origin.

Not all fire alarm boxes send a message to the fire department. That little red box in the hallway may do nothing more than ring the bell above it. Automatic sprinklers may only start the flow of water. If you don't know if an alarm notifies the fire department, *CALL*.

Once a sprinkler system activates, it's up to fire officials to deactivate it, not the security officer or other employees.

If you must send an employee out to the street to pull a fire alarm, send a second worker to follow a minute later in case something happens to the first. Both should then wait by the street alarm box to direct firefighters when they arrive.

Once people are out of the way and the alarm has been sounded, assess if the fire is beyond your control with simple extinguishers. If it is, then attempt to contain it. Fire feeds on fuel and oxygen. Close doors. Leave windows shut. Shut off air shafts, circulating fans, and air conditioners.

Ninety-five percent of fire-related deaths are due to smoke inhalation. Ventilation systems use smoke detectors to shut down the system so they don't spread the smoke. Smoke and heat rise so the safest place is with your nose to the floor. The movie scenes of firefighters rescuing children and crawling out of the building are accurate.

"Flash over" is a dramatic, frightening, and deadly effect. A fire smolders, and then begins to fill an area with smoke. The heat rises and flammable material in the room ignites simultaneously.

In 1961, the Hartford Hospital in Hartford, Connecticut,

A security officer checking fire equipment. Of all possible hazards, fire is the most potentially damaging to a company.

suffered a simple fire that started at an obstruction in the trash chute. No one noticed the hot duct or smelled the odor. A trash door on the ninth floor was not latched. It blew open and a fireball flew down the hallway. An ambulatory patient opened his door to see what happened and he was incinerated. He and 15 others died in that fire. Patients and staff whose doors remained closed survived.

Send people to stairwells. They're usually designed as fire escapes. If you must open a door, feel it first with the back of your hand to see if the surface is cool. Stay low and to the side when you turn the doorknob. If the fire does flash, it may pass over you.

The security officer's job isn't over when firefighters arrive. They will take charge of the fire—many states by law designate the senior fire official at the scene as in charge of all personnel. You know the area better than they do, however, so you can tell them the best route to get behind the fire and warn them of any hazardous materials and other dangers in the area.

If other security officers have joined you at this point, use them. Post officers at fire exits, at entrances that curious onlookers might use, at hydrants, at hoses to prevent vehicles from driving over them, and at the shelter area for personnel. If the facility has a restricted high-security area, perhaps the fire was deliberately set as a diversion. Consider sending additional security officers to sensitive posts.

Your job isn't over when the fire is out. Only your supervisor or replacement can relieve you from your post. You still need to keep people out of the fire area, admitting only arson investigators and fire officials. For safety reasons and for the success of the investigation, keep onlookers out of a fire damaged building. It's like protecting a crime scene. Nothing should be disturbed for fear of destroying evidence, including bodies. Mark the location and report it.

Finally, when it's all over, review your fire emergency plan and see how it can be improved.

Chapter 21
DANGEROUS DRUGS

A drug is any foreign substance that affects the physiological functions of the body. You may think that the illegal drug scene doesn't affect you. There's no question that drug and alcohol users are present on your employer's premises. The only question is how many are abusers.

The Controlled Substances Act defines drugs as:
Narcotics—opium, morphine, cocaine, heroin, and methadone.
Depressants—chloral hydrate, barbiturates, and methaqualone.
Stimulants—amphetamines, phenmetrazine, and methylphenidate.
Hallucinogens—LSD, mescaline and peyote, amphetamine variants, phencyclidine, and phencyclidine analogs.
Cannabis—marijuana, tetrahydrocannabinol, hashish, and hashish oil.

The act also schedules drugs according to their potential for abuse, potential for dependence, and medical value or use. Drugs included in Schedule I are those with high potential for abuse and no common medical value, such as heroin, marijuana, and LSD. Schedule II includes those with high potential for abuse and some medical value, such as opium and cocaine. All substances listed in Schedules I and II are illegal. Schedule III includes barbiturates and codeine; Schedule IV, phenobarbital and valium; and Schedule V is everything else. Penalties are assessed according to the schedule in which the drug is listed.

These drugs cause physical dependence, psychological dependence, or both. One who is "hooked" on drugs becomes obsessed with getting the next "fix." That next fix can be more important than the company's cash in the till, even more important than your life if you're standing in the way. Of all the inmates in prison, 65 to 70 percent are there because of a drug-related activity.

A drug-dependent employee will work hard to conceal the habit. At the same time, the abuser is building a tolerance and often needs larger doses of the drug over time to achieve the same effects.

Odd behavior is not necessarily connected with illegal drug use. Diabetics have a legitimate need for a syringe and needle. An employee's tablets or capsules could be a prescription, and sniffles and runny eyes could be hay fever. Even the experts may have difficulty making a proper diagnosis. Don't act on your own when you suspect an employee is "high." Take the subject to the company doctor. If you're not able to handle it internally and the subject is a threat (impaired driving ability or belligerence), turn the employee over to police.

Symptoms that may point to drug misuse by an employee are radical changes in work attendance, changes in normal abilities, inattention to dress and personal hygiene, unusual efforts to cover the arms (to hide needle marks), and association with known drug users.

Indicators of a user of intravenous narcotics are the "tracks" or needle marks on the arms, pinhole pupils, frequent scratching, and loss of appetite. The abuser may be drowsy after a fix, and restless with sniffles and watery eyes before the fix. The security officer can watch for a syringe, bent spoon, small metal bottle, glassine bags, or tinfoil packets on the subject's person.

Depressants cause behavior similar to alcohol intoxication, but without the odor of alcohol. Watch for sluggishness or difficulty in thinking and concentrating, slurred speech, faulty judgement, impaired motor skills, and falling asleep at work.

The effects of stimulants include exhilaration, hyperactivity, loss of appetite, repetitive non-purposeful behavior, dilated pupils, and chronically runny nose. Users may have straws, small spoons, mirrors, and razor blades in their possession.

Most hallucinogens cause wide shifts in behavior and mood. Users may sit quietly in a trance-like state, or appear terrified. They may experience nausea, chills, irregular breathing, sweating, and trembling of hands. Abusers of PCP

(Phencyclidine), an animal tranquilizer, are likely to be uncommunicative, exhibit a blank stare with eyes flicking from side to side, walk with a high stepping gait, have an increased insensitivity to pain, and experience amnesia.

Marijuana users exhibit signs of intoxication, lethargy, impaired motor skills, and a distorted sense of time and distance. This makes them a menace behind the wheel.

Chapter 22
BOMB THREATS

One phone call can throw your whole facility into a turmoil. You answer, "Security, Officer Clede." A voice responds, "I planted a bomb in your building. . ."

Most bomb threats are hoaxes—but not all. In 1990, 727 events occurred in which devices exploded, killing a total of 200 people, injuring 1,700, and causing $17 million in property damage. In a world of terrorism and political bombings, these calls cannot be dismissed as pranks. A number of steps must be taken immediately by the security officer.

First, deal with the caller. If there is a recorder on the phone line, turn it on. Stay calm. The caller wants to create turmoil and panic; remaining calm will help to keep the caller on the line while you evaluate the threat. Ask questions in a soothing voice, "Oh, why did you do that?" You might induce the caller to give a reason. Listen carefully. Take notes and record your impressions. How something was said may be as important as what was said. Be conversational, keep the caller on the line as long as possible so you can acquire more information. Listen for background noises that could help to place the caller's location.

Ask specific questions about the bomb. Is it a dynamite bomb? The caller may tell you, assuming you'll never see it anyway. Is it a time bomb? How is it triggered? Keep the caller talking. When is it set to go off?

Avoid asking questions such as, "Who is this?" The caller is not going to tell you and may hang up if you act angry.

Next, ask more direct questions. Where is the bomb? What does it look like? Where are you calling from? Ask anything that comes to mind to keep the conversation going. In your notes, describe the caller's voice, male or female, young or old, accent, tone of voice, and background noises. Did the voice sound familiar? It may be a disgruntled or former employee.

Report the call immediately to your supervisor, and only to

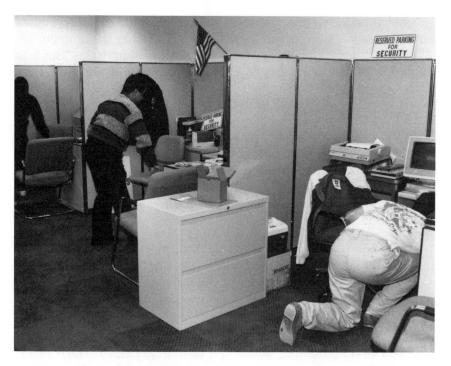

During this training class for security officers, a drill is conducted to find a bomb hidden in the building.

your supervisor. Follow the company's bomb threat plan. You don't want panic in the building.

EVACUATION

Better to be safe than sorry. Your plan probably begins with evacuating the building or area. You might start it as a "fire drill." Like a fire drill, tell people to use the stairs and not the elevators. If it's done by word of mouth, pass the message to supervisors of each department and let them handle their own people. But if no one is in charge of a room with 100 desks, don't waste time, announce the evacuation order. Appoint an employee to lead others to their designated standby area outside. Remember, calmness is contagious. Giving people directions reassures them. Before you declare an area clear, check the restrooms, stock rooms, and other out-of-the-way places.

"Just a minute," one obstinate worker retorts. Or, "I don't have time to waste on your silly drills." Don't waste time arguing. Approach closely and, in a soft but stern voice, simply say, "Sir, it is in your own best interest to do exactly as I have told you. NOW!"

SEARCHING FOR BOMBS

Your bomb plan should define the conduct of a search and who is in charge. It is important to follow procedures to the letter and do exactly as directed by the security supervisor.

Depending on how well the officer who took the call was able to perform, you may have some idea of what to look for. This is where observation skills are challenged. A bomb could resemble almost anything and be located almost anywhere. For example, look for a box out of place or a briefcase in an office when the occupant normally takes it home.

The device could look like any ordinary object. A bomb hidden in a portable radio blew up Pan Am flight 103 over Lockerbie, Scotland. Bombs can be as small as a pack of cigarettes and they don't all tick.

If you find something out of the ordinary, DON'T TOUCH IT. Movement sets off some types of bomb triggers. Report it to your supervisor. Also, don't stand over it and key the microphone on your portable radio—some bombs have radio-controlled detonators.

CROWD CONTROL

Once employees and others have left the premises, allow no one back in except authorized emergency personnel, until you are notified officially of the all clear. People in the assembly area must remain there, employees wandering around could interfere with emergency operations. If the crowd is in a public area, closely observe those gathered. Watch for anyone who doesn't belong—sometimes a bomber will try to watch the furor to see what happens when the device detonates. If you see someone suspicious, don't act on your own, call your supervisor or the police. A bomber could have a radio trigger for the bomb.

When you receive an all clear, direct the orderly re-entry of personnel in the same professional manner as you directed the evacuation. Don't leave them in the lurch now that they are accustomed to looking to you for leadership.

Chapter 23

CIVIL DISTURBANCES AND NATURAL DISASTERS

When workers strike, or radicals block the front gate, or power goes out, or nature unleashes a tornado or earthquake, it is likely there is an emergency plan available to guide you.

In general, disaster plans outline procedures for helping others, securing sensitive papers or materials, and moving people to shelter. Fire lanes must be kept open for emergency vehicles. Stay in contact with headquarters. One time, a tornado hit in a rural setting and no word came out of the disaster area from the responding officers. Several patrol cars had been sent to the scene, and it was as if they had dropped off the edge of the world. An officer's natural reaction is to stop and help. At such a time, it's more important to call for reinforcements or other emergency services first.

Providing information is also important during civil emergencies. A riot cannot be reacted to unless your supervisors know what they are dealing with. For instance, most riots start as a small group of angry people. The security officer is trained to deal with small groups, and your composure and helpful authority could defuse the situation. If the situation escalates and turns into a riot, it will take a solid line of confident officers to control the situation.

Control your temper in a riot situation. When cursed at, think, "I'm a professional and I love my job." Ignore distractions and stay calm. Throw your shoulders back and project an aura of strength and authority. Give orders when necessary, but never argue with, threaten, or try to bluff anyone. Watch out for the other officers; everyone likes to know their back is being watched.

It's beyond the scope of this book to go into riot control tactics.

You're no longer acting as an individual officer during riot conditions, you are part of a security team. If you are told to form a line to contain a crowd or go into a wedge formation to break up a mob, your supervisor has reasons for ordering this. Watch for the instigators or leaders. Separate the individual who's inciting the crowd. This might break up the riot.

Terrorists are a different matter. Report any rumors of terrorism. Prevention is better than apprehension. You need to cautiously investigate anything out of the ordinary. If you suspect terrorist activity, call for back up. Terrorists are trained in taking out the lonely guard, and they rarely act alone.

Chapter 24

INVESTIGATION

The basic job of the security officer is investigation—even if your post is simply standing guard. It is through investigation that "institutional security deficiencies" are identified.

Les Williams Jr., retired from the Connecticut State Police, now brings his experience to others by teaching. Much of his teaching is to security officers and one of the first subjects he covers is investigation.

Investigation is the collection of facts, gathered in an organized manner, and preserved so as to be legally admissible in court.

The purposes of a security officer's investigation are:
1. To identify the guilty party and the events which occurred.
2. To locate the guilty party or cause of the problem.
3. To provide evidence of guilt or cause to management who must then decide the next step.

TOOLS

Williams classifies the tools of investigation into three categories:

Information—gathered from talking to people and examining objects.

Interview or Interrogation—talking with someone who knows something you don't. You interview a cooperative witness, someone who wants to help. You interrogate an uncooperative person who may want to mislead you.

Instrumentation—the application of physical science to gather information from objects. Although the forensic sciences could fill a series of books, the basics will be discussed here so you can properly preserve evidence gathered during your investigation.

SUCCESSFUL INVESTIGATION

A successful investigation must satisfy these criteria:
1. All available physical evidence is competently handled.
2. All witnesses are intelligently interviewed.
3. Suspects are effectively interrogated and given a chance to tell their side of the story.
4. All leads are properly developed.

Are good investigators "born" or "made"? Although good investigators are born, they can also be made if they understand what they are doing. Investigation is more than a list of procedures or a matter of following specific techniques. Investigators need a natural curiosity to recognize what could be an unusual lead. This means they must understand people, products, situations, and circumstances.

It's easy to see why a recruit doesn't begin a career in the investigative division. The security officer learns investigative skills in training, but these skills are fully developed only with experience. However, even recruits can influence the effectiveness of an investigation by their actions at the scene and the reports they write.

CRIME SCENE

The security officer is often first on the scene of a crime. The chapter on Scene Protection and Search offers a long list of things to do and not to do. The initial actions taken by the officer at the scene can determine the success of the subsequent investigation.

For instance, an office worker returns from lunch and finds the office in a shambles. When you answer the call, the occupant wants to march around to show the disruption. A rear window was broken and entered, so you go out and get a good look from outside. In the course of these innocent meanderings, valuable evidence could be destroyed.

Procedures for various types of crime scenes should be part of your training. Be aware that the first officer to arrive at a crime scene is faced with a great responsibility.

If there are victims, do they need first aid? Was a crime

committed? First, notify the dispatcher of your evaluation of the situation. Request medical assistance or render first aid if needed. While you're doing this, remember to preserve any potential physical evidence such as footprints and fingerprints. Next, your job is to secure and protect the scene. Identify possible witnesses. Be aware that a perpetrator might return, or may still be present. Until a supervisor arrives, the officer who was dispatched to the call is in charge. Establish a perimeter and direct spectators where to stand. Delegate this responsibility to another employee, if you must, but keep people's feet and curious hands out of any area that might contain evidence.

Even if it's the company president, insist, "I'm sure you do not want to jeopardize the success of this investigation. We'd appreciate your cooperation." Police departments have special units of trained crime scene investigators, and the responding patrol officer keeps even other officers out of the scene. If there are entrances to the area that you can't cover, have another security officer block access. Nothing must be disturbed. Once you have identified possible physical evidence, remember that responding police units, supervisors, ambulances, paramedics, and investigators don't know where it is. Be present to direct them and prevent potential destruction of evidence. Normally, a crime scene investigator will survey the area to determine safe pathways where officers and medics may walk without destroying evidence. But if there is a need for medical attention on the scene before the investigator arrives, determine the least destructive routes.

Even seemingly simple scenes can turn up surprising information. Lt. Robert L. Burriss heads the forensic investigations unit of the Biloxi, Mississippi, police department. He illustrates how a qualified investigator can learn from a crime scene.

After a local store was burglarized, Burriss searched the interior and found nothing. When examining the crime scene photos, he noticed a dolly leaning against the wall outside the rear entrance. A dolly is not unusual, but outside? The owner confirmed that the dolly was kept inside. Burriss dusted it for fingerprints and lifted a perfect set. Eventually, he made a match. Police followed up and found merchandise from the store in the home of the suspect. The "out of place" or "unusual" could be as simple as this.

Burriss is convinced that crime scenes "talk" to him, if he looks and listens hard enough.

In another case, a woman was found shot to death in an automobile. Her husband admitted he shot her, but said it was accidental—they were struggling for the gun. Burriss worked the scene. He found blood spattered on the husband, almost none in the car, and a few drops on the ground beside the car. Burriss wasn't satisfied. The next day he visited the funeral home and examined the body. A bruise had appeared on her face and another on her arm as if fingers had gripped it. Burriss wondered.

The husband's story was that he had grappled with the woman over the gun. But that would occupy both hands, Burriss thought. He examined the car again. The blood inside was a soaking stain, rather than a spatter you'd find from a gunshot wound. A blood spatter had been found on the ground outside of the car. Burriss deduced the husband had pulled his wife from the car, shot her, then put her back into the car. Confronted with the evidence, the husband confessed.

Events happen fast when you arrive at a crime scene. Burriss' advice is to compose yourself before going in, and log everything you do so you can advise the forensic investigator when he or she arrives. Keep people away, seal the scene as quickly as possible, and don't touch or move anything.

A murder weapon was given to a department firearms instructor to check for functioning and safety. As it happened, the instructor understood that biological material can be blown back into the bore of a gun from a contact wound. Even though he wasn't asked, he ran a dry patch through the bore and filed it away for later possible use as evidence. Then he performed the tests requested.

Bullets can't always be matched to the responsible gun with a comparison microscope. The problem in this case was that the evidence bullet was badly deformed, so there was no way to link the gun to the victim. There was a good chance of losing the case until the instructor heard this in a chance conversation. He suggested an analysis of the dry patch he had run through the barrel. The lab found trace evidence of blood and tissue that matched the victim. If the firearms instructor had done only what was asked of him, and not taken the extra step to preserve evidence, the case would have been unsolved.

SHOOTING CASES

Lucien C. Haag of Phoenix, Arizona, was technical director and criminologist at the Phoenix police department crime lab for nearly 17 years. Now he heads Forensic Science Services, Inc. and consults around the world. He has published more than 60 scientific papers, mostly concerned with exterior and terminal ballistics and the effects and behavior of projectiles. He is a past president of the Association of Firearms and Toolmark Examiners.

Haag is particularly interested in the reconstruction of shooting scenes. "My biggest grievance over the years has been the misplaced concern many officers have that the gun lying on the floor at a shooting scene is suddenly going to strike out and injure someone unless there's a mad rush to make it safe and unload it."

In one case, a man lay dead on the floor of a Phoenix bar, one bullet hole in his body. Another person was standing over him holding a literally smoking gun from which three shots had been fired. Everyone else in the room was "in the bathroom" when the shots were fired. On the scene, the responding police officer drew a picture of the cylinder and cartridge locations.

The only witness both living and willing to testify was the suspect. He claimed the deceased was the aggressor who, intoxicated, had come at him with a broken beer bottle. The suspect explained that he had fired a warning shot into the ceiling, and another into the floor, and a third and final shot into the aggressor.

At it happens, bullets were recovered from the ceiling (a Winchester), the floor (a Remington), and the body (a Federal). According to the field officer's diagram, a Winchester case was in cylinder position one, a Remington in two, and a Federal in three. Other mixed unfired brands were in the remaining three. Haag says mixed brands are common in such shootings.

Knowing where the cartridges were in the cylinder could substantiate the defendant's statement. What if the Winchester bullet had been recovered from the body? The diagram would have shown the subject had fired first at the victim and the other two shots were either wild shots or were fired to set up his self-defense story. If the responding officer had hurriedly opened the revolver and dumped the cylinder's contents into his hand, no one would ever know whether the suspect was telling the truth.

"All officers need to understand the variety of firearms evidence that can be important, beyond the simple matching of a fired bullet to the gun that fired it," Haag says. "Given the variety of ammunition, bullets, and propellants used in shootings, there are ways to determine not only who fired a particular shot, but how the shooting occurred—who fired first, from which direction or position, how many shots were fired, and in what sequence." Which shot was fired last was critical in that barroom case. Possible issues regarding ricochet or deflection can become a vital factor that doesn't emerge until later.

"Rather than just putting things in envelopes and routing them to the lab with the usual request to match the bullet to the gun, there needs to be much earlier communication between the investigator and the forensic firearms examiner. It takes this dialogue to pinpoint what the issues really are, and to determine how to prioritize analytical procedures," according to Haag.

In another case, a man called police and said he had just accidentally shot his wife. Officers found the woman dead from a single gunshot wound to her chest. A Smith & Wesson Model 39 autoloading pistol was found on a nearby dresser. A loaded magazine was later recovered from under the mattress, after the husband told the police where to find it. The husband said that the pistol and magazine were always kept apart, that the magazine was not in the pistol when the accident occurred.

The husband explained that he got the pistol from a nightstand drawer when he heard a noise outside. He didn't think there was a cartridge in the chamber and had started toward the bed to get the magazine when he must have inadvertently touched the trigger. Hearing his wife cry out, he immediately set the pistol on the dresser and rushed to her aid.

Understanding the mechanism of the suspect gun, an officer would know that the Model 39 has a magazine disconnector. If it were in good working order, it could not fire without a magazine inserted. Suppose blood traces were found on the second cartridge down in the magazine? The suspect obviously removed the live round from the pistol and put it back into the magazine before he placed it under the mattress and called police.

Preserving the magazine just as it was found and getting blood samples of those involved would be critical. With recent forensic developments, blood traces can be matched with "almost fingerprint specificity" to a person.

The careful diagramming of a shooting scene can be critical in determining the distance the shooter was from the victim at the moment of discharge. For instance, the victim's garments can be tested for gunshot residue patterns—if the medics don't throw them away—and then a test of the gun at the distance claimed can produce a gunshot residue pattern that can be compared with the suspect's story.

There is a lot more to firearms evidence than is seen on cop shows on television, and it involves many details other than the gun itself. When you are the first responder to a crime scene involving guns, you must anticipate the possible questions attorneys might raise to discredit the case. Getting the forensic expert involved early can help. If these questions come as a surprise when you are on the witness stand, it's too late to decide which tests should have been performed to substantiate your case.

COUNTERFEITING

The counterfeiting of currency is one of the oldest crimes in history. With the convenience of modern photography and printing techniques, counterfeiting is again on the rise.

When employees are concerned about a bill they receive, the first person they are likely to ask about it is the security officer. You should understand what bills are in circulation and how to spot a counterfeit.

There are three types of U.S. paper currency in circulation today. Federal Reserve notes have a green seal and serial number, and are in denominations of $1, $2, $5, $10, $20, $50, and $100. U.S. notes have a red seal and serial number and are in denominations of $2, $5, and $100. Silver certificates have a blue seal and number, and were in denominations of $1, $5, and $10. Silver certificates, as well as $2 and $5 U.S. notes, are no longer printed. The $100 bill is the highest denomination now being printed.

The best way to detect a counterfeit bill is to compare it with a genuine bill of the same denomination and series. Look for the red and blue fibers in the paper. Counterfeiters try to mimic these fibers by printing colored lines on the paper. There are new issue bills with bars containing microscopic printing.

Look for differences, not similarities. The counterfeit bill is usually printed by a photomechanical process and is not as sharp as the real thing. It may appear flat, lacking the three-dimensional quality of genuine bills. In the portrait background, the lines form squares. On counterfeits, some squares may be filled in, and delicate lines in the portrait may be broken or missing. The portrait is lifeless and the background is usually too dark. Sawtooth points on the seal are usually uneven, blunt, or broken off. Serial numbers may be off color, improperly spaced or aligned. Border lines that crisscross are not clear and distinct.

Any counterfeit bill you find is contraband, so you must seize it. Then follow the policy of your employer.

WORKING UNDERCOVER

Working undercover is a special assignment experienced by a very few officers. In your career as a security officer, you will become acquainted with many police officers. Remember that recognizing an officer working undercover at the wrong time could be hazardous to the officer's health. If you are involved in an undercover operation involving your company, every security officer needs to know just enough about it to avoid jeopardizing a fellow officer.

What happens if you stumble onto a drug buy? You probably won't recognize an undercover officer, but if you do—hide it. If he happened to be a close friend and you say, "Hi, Joe," he could wind up dead. If you take any action, treat him the same as everyone else.

Chapter 25
SURVEILLANCE

A security officer has a wider latitude of actions with fewer restrictions than a police officer. A police department is an agency of the government needing a warrant to trespass on private property, tap telephone lines, or use electronic devices to intercept conversations which involved persons would reasonably expect to be free of government intrusion. As a security officer, you have a right to be on the private property where you're employed. You may use company provided closed-circuit television to watch sensitive locations. Under company rules, an employee may be subject to a search on entering or leaving a sensitive area.

However, the security officer must be aware of constraints on police, because a case may develop to the point that it is turned over to police. If your investigation is "clean," the job for police is easier.

EXPECTATION OF PRIVACY

Security officers may conduct a surveillance using unaided eyes and ears anywhere, unless it invades a suspect's reasonable expectation of privacy.

It is important that you understand this concept. Even certain public places may give the person utilizing them an expectation of privacy. Observation into a bathroom stall from an overhead vantage point, or looking through an overhead vent into a motel room, has been held as unreasonable invasion of privacy. Remember the difference between "curtilage" and "open fields." If you walk onto the lawn and look into the window, that is an unreasonable invasion of privacy. Observation from an adjacent open field or from the street is not.

If people conduct themselves in a way that disregards privacy, they may be subject to observation even in a private home. A domestic dispute in an apartment may be overheard by an officer standing in the hallway—the couple has no reasonable expectation of privacy. A suspect running a numbers game in his garage has no reasonable expectation of privacy from police who are able to look into the garage window from a nearby railroad track. The principle involved here is that the officers have a right to be on the railroad track.

On the other hand, people may lose their expectation of privacy in a public place if there is reason to believe they are not using it for the purpose for which it was intended. For example, two men went into the restroom at a gas station and remained there for more than a half hour. The attendant called police, who entered with a passkey. That entry was held to be reasonable, and the drug paraphernalia seized was admitted into evidence at the trial.

ELECTRONIC SURVEILLANCE

The use of electronic devices for surveillance is strictly regulated. Without a court order (except in limited emergency situations), it is a serious federal offense. It is difficult to write black and white rules about the correct use of electronic surveillance, but here are comments on past court decisions.

Using an extension phone is not a tap if the subscriber on the other extension permits it. However, some states have more stringent rules requiring two-party consent in the absence of a court order. Electronic surveillance conducted on the order of a state or local judge is illegal under federal law unless there is specific state law authorizing the judge to issue such an order.

However, in most but not all states, federal and state officers may electronically overhear or intercept conversations if they have the consent of one of the parties. For instance, if you "wire" an informer who enters a suspect's home, you may overhear and record conversations between the suspect and the informer. By the same token, you can listen in on a telephone conversation if you have the consent of one of the parties. In both cases, the suspect has "misplaced his confidence" in the informer and has no reasonable expectation of privacy. In some states you must have the consent of both parties.

There are fewer restrictions on the use of devices that do not intercept communications. Using a pen register on phone company property to record the number the subscriber dials is not protected in some states, although others require a court order. The subscriber has no expectation of privacy in the numbers dialed. This also applies to devices that identify the phone numbers of incoming calls to a particular phone.

The use of electronic location devices, or beepers, is a gray area. Police don't need a warrant to attach a beeper to the outside of a vehicle, but may need one to install it inside. If police have consent to put a beeper in an object, they don't need a warrant before delivering the bugged package to an unsuspecting person. However, they will need a warrant to continue monitoring if the beeper is taken into a private place. As this is written, the Supreme Court had addressed beeper monitoring in only two contexts: on the open road and in a home.

Chapter 26
SCENE PROTECTION AND SEARCH

The security officer will often be the first responder to the scene of a crime or accident. Any action taken at that time will influence the case all the way through the criminal justice system.

After tending to the injured, putting out the fire, and identifying and detaining witnesses, the security officer will politely ask bystanders to leave in order to preserve critical evidence, as described in the chapter on Investigation. This is scene protection.

The purpose of a crime-scene investigation is to reconstruct events that led up to the commission of a crime. Significant evidence might be anything from a single hair to an automobile, from skin flecks under a victim's fingernails to a gun.

Identify the complainant if there is one. Then, identify all those present when the event occurred or who might have knowledge of it. Your employer's investigator or the police will need to interview them later.

In a situation in which several witnesses are present, separate them to prevent discussion of the sequence of events. No two people ever see the same things the same way. Each person sees part of it. The follow-up interview will determine what each witness actually saw. It's the investigator's job to put the pieces together into one whole picture.

An example: An audio-visual (TV and VCR) unit was stolen from inside the locked projection booth in the company conference room. It had to have happened sometime between Friday evening, after the person with the key locked up, and Monday morning when it was found missing. The security officer searched the area and confirmed that both projection booth and conference room doors were locked the entire time. No evidence of tampering was found. The security officer concluded it was an "inside job" and so stated in the report.

The investigator followed up on the report. The keyholder was interviewed. The investigator performed a spiral search of the conference room and found nothing. During a thorough search of the projection booth the investigator found a little dust by the inside wall adjacent to the hallway. A search of the hallway showed a sneaker print on a hall table exactly opposite of where the dust inside the booth was found. The investigator then examined the ceiling and found the dust disturbed. Some dust had fallen into the booth when the thief slid a ceiling panel aside to drop into the booth. By finding faint traces of evidence, the investigator reconstructed the theft. Another employee stood on the hall table and pushed a ceiling panel aside, hoisted up and over the wall, and gained access to the booth through another panel. The secured locks were bypassed.

Consider the consequences had this investigator not determined the facts of the case. The responsible keyholder who was innocent may well have been fired.

The point is—never jump to conclusions. Otherwise, you will gather only the evidence that supports your conclusion. You don't really know what happened until after the evidence is gathered and you have taken time to consider all possibilities.

There are five steps to an investigation:

1. Shoot overall photos of the scene. This is a visual record of what the situation was before anything was disturbed. Diagram the scene, literally draw a plot of the area, noting location of doors and windows.
2. Note the conditions you found when you arrived and describe them. Were wall hangings out of place or disturbed, for instance?
3. Search the area systematically. You might choose one of three search methods. One is the **strip method**, where you work your way back and forth as you move across the room. The **zone method** involves breaking the area up into grid. The **spiral method** begins at one point and circles as you would mow the front lawn.

Look for anything out of the ordinary. In the case cited above, one critical piece of evidence was dust on the floor of the booth beside the interior wall. Don't assume the significance or insignificance of any evidence when you first find it.

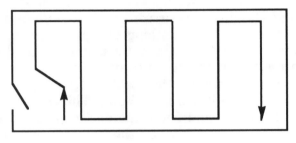

Strip Method

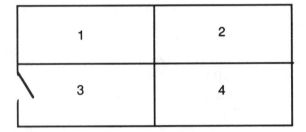

Zone Method

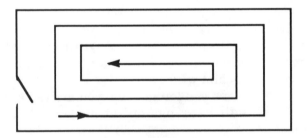

Spiral Method

4. Once you have documented evidence and conducted interviews with witnesses, evaluate your findings. Given the witnesses' statements, what should you have found but did not? If something you expected is missing, perhaps your search was not thorough enough or the search area was not

properly defined. If a weapon is missing, which way would the perpetrator most likely have gone? Is there a dumpster along the way?

5.   Now begin to reconstruct the incident.

First, be confident that you will find something important during the search. Use all your senses. For instance, reading is educational, but put the same story on television and you get more out of it. Why? Because you now see and hear it. Put it on stage and it's even better because you now see, hear, and smell. If you could get on stage with the actors, you could see, hear, smell, and feel. Why does a baby put everything it picks up into its mouth? Taste is part of learning about things. Remember, use all of your senses.

Every crime scene search is a team effort. But, if there is more than one security person at a scene, one person must be in charge. Depending on personnel available, designate a photographer, a sketcher, a note taker, and an evidence collector. If your security department has a special investigative unit, there may be an officer trained for each job.

COLLECTING EVIDENCE

Physical evidence is any material that aids in identifying the situation, the person involved, or the cause of the incident. Everything in the world leaves a trail, or traces, of its existence. When any object touches another, a transfer of material takes place. Fingerprints, for instance, are caused by oils on the skin that transfer an image of the pattern of ridges and whorls from the fingertip to the object the finger touched. Other physical evidence left by the human body may include hairs, spittle, perspiration, or other fluids. Dust or mud from a shoe leaves its mark, as on the hallway table in the case cited earlier. Fabric traces might consist of a strand rather than a fragment of cloth.

The point is that important evidence may be microscopic in size. I recall a rape case where the victim could not identify the exact spot in the woods where the crime happened. She never got a good look at the rapist. Police brought in a body search dog and soon located the scene. Then the evidence technicians took over. They actually found traces of semen which, through DNA "fingerprinting," were identified as belonging to the accused.

Everything you find must be identified in some way. Attach a tag to large objects or use a stick-on label after the fingerprint experts have cleared it. Put small objects into plastic bags and label the bag. Labels or tags should list the case number, location, date and time found, investigating officer, and any other remarks. Remember to mark the crime scene sketch with the item number to show where it was found.

"Chain of custody" is a term you'll hear in relation to all evidence. How does a judge know that the evidence presented in court is actually what was found and is in the same condition as when it was found? For instance, the responding security officer found the gun, a responding police officer bagged it, gave it to his sergeant, who gave it to the lieutenant, who took it to headquarters and gave it to the evidence room officer. The longer the chain, the weaker the evidence. Even if it's a minor case kept within the company, the aggrieved could file suit and you would have to present the evidence to justify your or the company's actions.

For evidence to be admissible in court, the officer must prove that it was properly handled all along the way. Here are six steps to insuring admissible evidence:

1. **Protection.** The evidence was guarded at the scene to prevent tampering.

2. **Collection.** Material was properly bagged without disturbing trace evidence it might hold. Here's where most errors occur. If you collect a soil sample contaminated with a possible accelerant, for example, you should also collect a sample of untainted soil so the lab technicians can compare them. The control sample is the "known." When you subtract that from the evidence sample, you are left with only the questionable.

3. **Identification.** The evidence was given a distinctive mark or number to designate that particular thing from a million others in the world.

4. **Preservation.** Evidence was safeguarded in possession, or under lock and key and only you have the key. Each additional person assigned to safeguard evidence lengthens the chain of custody.

5. **Transmission.** Log every step of the path the evidence follows. From person to person, into and out of the safe, keep a complete record of everything that happens to the evidence from discovery to presentation in court.

6. **Disposition.** Evidence remains evidence until the case is settled, and sometimes longer. Never dispose of evidence without clearance from the court or someone of responsibility. Open but dormant cases have been reinvestigated using new technology on the evidence and have been solved. President Zachery Taylor's body was recently exhumed to test hair and bone fragments for evidence of arsenic. His death certificate says the cause of death was gastroindocrinitis, but a writer's theory was that he was poisoned. Testing found that he had died of natural causes.

Chapter 27
WEAPONS ARE YOUR RESPONSIBILITY

The security officer uses many tools, including weapons. Whatever the weapon, you are responsible for using it properly.

BEING MENTALLY PREPARED

If you are armed, how many firearms instructors have preached that the handgun is simply a tool of the trade? That the odds are you'll never need to use it?

"An officer was called to a situation where there was known danger. He heard shots fired. He continued moving in, the gun still in his holster. The killer saw him first. The officer died with his gun still strapped in its leather." Massad Ayoob, director of the Lethal Force Institute, tells that story to prove the point: If you're mentally unprepared to exert deadly force, your gun is not an effective weapon.

Your company has put you in position as its protector, using whatever force and weapons are necessary and justified. That means you may have to kill. The shooting decision isn't made by the officer. It's a reaction to the circumstances presented to the officer by the assailant. You shoot only to stop "the aggressor's felonious action that endangers himself or another," but the aftermath is a death by your hand.

NEVER GIVE UP

When you played hide and seek or cops and robbers as a kid the rules of the game required that if you were tagged, you gave up. When you participate in shooting scenarios during officer survival training and don't shoot a hostile target, you are scored "dead." We continue to play by the same old rules. But it is necessary to add a new consideration. Four out of five shootings do not result in incapacitation. That's why firearms instructors teach the "double tap," or placing two rounds into the target in rapid succession. The odds are that, even if you are shot, you can take out the shooter—if you are mentally prepared to be shot.

TAKE OFFENSE

It's offensive if someone shoots you, so take offense. Get angry, but control your anger so you can be cool and calculated in your response. After all, the shooter has tried to deprive you of everything you hold dear. As long as the offender holds a gun and is capable of pulling the trigger, he'll keep trying. You are seen as an obstacle preventing escape, and removing the obstacle is a natural act to ensure the offender's survival. You have no alternative. You must stop the aggressor's felonious act in the way you were trained.

FIREARMS SAFETY

Wearing a gun has a sobering influence on an officer. Your responses are more reserved than if you did not have a gun. You are careful to avoid aggravating situations. Yet, you must wear that gun with all the ease and comfort of wearing a key ring. You never "play" with it, nor show it off. You practice with an instructor on the range to become proficient in defensive shooting skills.

You can tell who's "expert" with a gun by the way it is handled. The gun is always considered loaded, whether it actually is or not. Experts never point at anything or anybody they don't intend to shoot. Unless actually shooting or holstered, the expert keeps the action open so the gun cannot fire. If you practice informally, you must know where your bullet is going to go—beyond the target.

If you have an armed security job, you must complete a firearms training course that includes all of these considerations, plus marksmanship and making shooting decisions.

GUN GRABS ARE A THREAT

While most security officers are not armed, it is important that all be trained in firearms retention. These techniques were developed to protect your handgun or shotgun from an assailant, or to retrieve it if a grab is successful. If someone sticks a gun in your face, knowing these techniques can get their gun into your hands in less than two seconds.

According to the FBI Uniform Crime Reports, 106 police officers were killed in 1979—17 with their own guns. The total number of officers feloniously killed declined steadily from 1979 to 1984. In 1984, the total of 72 was the lowest since 1968. But 12 of those 72 were killed with their own guns. In 1990, only 65 police officers were feloniously killed in the line of duty. That's the lowest total since the FBI began collecting these statistics in the 1960s. There are no data for security officers.

In Kansas City, Missouri, in one 18-month period, there were nine cases of police officers being disarmed. One officer was killed. One was shot in the leg. One was brutally beaten by an assailant who later killed a cab driver with the officer's revolver. "We evaluated and classified every case we could get a history on to determine how they happened and to develop a training program to respond to the most frequent circumstances," according to James Lindell, physical training supervisor for the police department.

Lindell, also a martial arts expert, is lanky and lithe. His graying hair belies what he can do to you with just his hands, arms, and feet. But Lindell is expert enough to know that not all officers behind the badge have the physique or motivation to become black belts. Experimenting with different martial arts techniques, and by trial and error, Lindell developed a simplified system aimed at defending the officer's revolver.

Years ago, the Kansas City police adopted Lindell's initial revolver retention system, and it continues to evolve and improve. Over the first five years of the program, in some 30 cases of disarming attempts, not one was successful. During the second five years, five officers were disarmed, but incident review determined that none had used personal defense, their weapon, or handgun retention techniques. Fortunately, none were injured, but each committed some procedural violation or was physically outmatched by a much stronger aggressor. The fact that none of these five used any of the defensive skills they learned in the academy states a strong case for at least annual refresher courses.

I won't try to summarize Lindell's entire 81-page training manual. You can obtain it from Odin Press, Box 11688, Kansas City, MO 64138.

THREE STEPS TO KEEPING YOUR HANDGUN

The Handgun Retention Course boils down to three simple steps: (1) secure the gun, (2) position, and (3) release.

The assailant is intent on grabbing your gun; the gun is the target. So, first secure the gun in the holster with one hand as you position yourself to provide protection for the gun and leverage against the attacker.

Keeping it simple, Lindell applies just five techniques that respond to virtually all the possible attempts to grab a holstered gun. If your gun is drawn, there are just four techniques you need to know, and they virtually ensure that you will keep control of your gun. Even if the assailant gets your gun out of the holster, there are three techniques that, in slightly more than a second, will retrieve the gun.

This simple three-step procedure uses wrist locks (jujitsu), blocks (karate), and throws (judo.) You don't need to know the physics of body mechanics, leverage, or nerves to apply these principles.

The secret is to first learn the fundamentals properly, then practice, practice, practice. It's like drawing the revolver. With practice, when the occasion arises, a well-trained officer's response takes place without conscious thought.

One of Lindell's students tells a story: "I felt the grab on my gun and, the next thing I knew, the guy was on the ground and my gun was in my hand aimed right at his temple." That's training!

KEEPING YOUR SHOTGUN

Consider a situation in which an officer with a shotgun faces a warehouse building search. A honeycomb of aisles and passages interlace the pallets of crates and boxes on the warehouse floor.

"That's one of the four situations where an attempt to disarm the officer with a shotgun is likely to occur," says Robert K. Lindsey. Lindsey, a retired captain from the Jefferson Parish, Louisiana, sheriff's department, is a training consultant. "The other situations are when the shotgun malfunctions, when you're reloading, and when you're in a 'don't shoot' situation."

Lindsey conducted a study of shotgun retention, and he has extensively studied officer survival.

"The usual self-defense techniques, by themselves, are not the answer to retaining the long gun," Lindsey says. Using his knowledge of defensive tactics and the martial arts, Lindsey developed four simple procedures that virtually ensure that you retain the shotgun, whether an assailant tries to grab it (1) from the front or off side, (2) from the strong side, (3) from the front with the gun at port arms, or (4) from the rear. His shoulder weapon retention system is outlined here, but, as in all defensive tactics, it should be learned and practiced under the guidance of a qualified instructor.

GRAB FROM THE FRONT OR SIDE

Imagine you are standing at a corner in a hallway. The subject steps out, grabs your shotgun, and tries to pull it away. Use the force of the subject's pull to your own advantage. React immediately by stepping forward with your off foot. Thrust the barrel toward the attacker. Then quickly step forward with your strong foot, forcing the butt of the gun downward. Next step past the attacker with your off foot while thrusting the barrel toward the outside of the attacker's body, and reach. You now have the gun. The final move is to distance yourself from the attacker. Get out of reach so the gun can't be grabbed again.

GRAB FROM THE REAR

This is a backward application of the grab from front or side technique. Immediately step backward with your strong foot, thrusting the butt downward and toward the outside. Pivot toward the attacker, while shoving the barrel toward the outside of the attacker's body. Then, step back and to the side with your strong foot, pulling the gun in close to yourself. You now have the gun, distance yourself from the attacker.

GRAB WHEN GUN MALFUNCTIONS

The subject sees that your gun is jammed and takes advantage of your predicament. Quickly rack the action back, wipe the shell away, and close the action. By that time, your gun is in the port arms position and the aggressor has his hands on it. Just follow the appropriate sequence above.

"With a shotgun, you must be continually aware of your surroundings. Weapon retention is enhanced by being alert and ready to react instantly and instinctively," Lindsey says. "Never allow an attacker to get a death grip on your gun."

Whether your job requires you to be armed or not, these techniques are important. They could also provide the means for you to disarm an assailant.

APPENDIX—ORGANIZATIONS

There are many associations aimed at aiding various police and security specialties in the exchange of information, improving professional skills, or refining new techniques. Membership organizations usually publish a magazine or newsletter, hold an annual convention, and provide other training and assistance to its members. Also included are organizations that might be helpful to security professionals.

American Society for Industrial Security
1655 North Fort Myer Drive #1200
Arlington, VA 22209
Phone 703-522-5800

ASIS was founded in 1955 to foster professionalism in the field of security. It sponsors the Certified Protection Professional (CPP) program for those who have met education and experience requirements and who have passed a written test. Contact Sue Melnicove.

American Society of Law Enforcement Trainers
P.O. Box 1003
Twin Lakes, WI 53181-1103
Phone 414-279-5700, E-Mail CompuServe 71630,2064

ASLET is a group of law enforcement trainers, educators, and administrators. Its purpose is to advance progressive and innovative law enforcement training. Edward Nowicki, executive director.

American Society for Training and Development
1640 King Street, Box 1443
Alexandria, VA 22313
Phone 703-683-8100

While not strictly a security training group, ASTD is the world's largest association in the field of employer-based training. It represents some 50,000 professionals.

Associated Public-Safety Communications Officers, Inc.
P.O. Box 669
New Smyrna Beach, FL 32069
Phone 904-427-3461

APCO works for the improvement of all forms of public safety communications. Founded in 1935, it is open to those employed by a public safety agency or company that provides products or service to the field. Bob Buttgen, executive director.

International Association of Airport & Seaport Police
580-2755 Lougheed Highway
Port Coquiltlam
British Columbia
Canada V3B 5Y9
Phone 604-942-2132, Fax 604-942-1755, Telex 053-3723

Airports and seaports worldwide face similar problems. Through international communication, cooperation, and consultation, IAASP works to improve operational effectiveness of airport and seaport law enforcement officers. Its objectives are to prevent and detect crime, study and recommend uniform practices for safeguarding international cargo, exchange information among law enforcement agencies and encourage cooperation among various sections of the international trade community for improved security. IAASP has 205 members in 40 countries and now maintains a full-time secretariat with T. Ciunyk as executive director.

International Association of Arson Investigators
25 Newton Street, P.O. Box 600
Marlboro, MA 01752

IAAI, founded in 1951, is dedicated to the control of arson and related crimes. Membership is open to those engaged in arson investigation, detection, and prosecution in the public or private sector. Contact Dan Lemieux.

International Association of Campus Law Enforcement Administrators
638 Prospect Avenue
Hartford, CT 06105
Phone 203-233-4531

IACLEA is dedicated to promoting professional ideals and standards of campus security and law enforcement. Membership is composed of colleges and universities throughout the United States, Canada and Mexico, individual campus law enforcement directors and staff, as well as criminal justice faculty and municipal police chiefs.

International Association of Credit Card Investigators
1620 Grant Avenue
Novato, CA 94947
Phone 415-897-8800

IACCI was formed in 1968 by a group of credit card investigators and law enforcement professionals to aid in the establishment of effective card and check safety programs, to suppress fraudulent use of cards and traveler's checks, and to detect and aid in the apprehension of violators. Membership classification is determined by the relationship of the applicant to the investigative function. D. D. Drummond, executive director.

International Association for Hospital Security and Safety
P.O. Box 637
Lombard IL 60148
Phone 708-953-0990

Founded in 1968, IAHSS is the largest association of its kind. It fosters the exchange of information and cooperation, and provides educational programs and publications pertinent to protecting a modern medical facility.

International Association of Law Enforcement Firearms Instructors
390 Union Avenue
Union Square
Laconia, NH 03246
Phone 603-524-8787, Fax 603-524-8856, E-Mail CompuServe 70031,1166

IALEFI was formed in October 1981 by firearms instructors to promote more relevant firearms training programs and enhance instructor skills. It publishes a quarterly magazine and sets criteria for training programs and instructor certification. Robert Bossey, executive director.

International Bodyguard Association
9842 Hibert Street #161
San Diego, CA 92131

IBA is a new organization for protective service agents throughout the world. It requires one year of experience with a federal, state, or local government agency, or a private agency as a protective services specialist. Its purpose is to advance the knowledge of the protective service agent, to maintain high standards and ethics, to promote efficiency of protective service agents and the services they perform, to aid in establishing effective security programs, and to emphasize a professional approach to the bodyguard function. The annual member directory provides international contacts. James A. King, executive director.

National Association of Investigative Specialists
P.O. Box 33244
Austin, TX 78764
Phone 512-832-0355, Fax 512-832-9376, E-Mail CompuServe 76050,3601

NAIS is a national trade association for professional licensed private investigators. It publishes a bi-monthly newsletter, a semi-annual membership directory, and more than 100 training manuals and courses. It runs a travel club, and an online network called PICON. Ralph D. Thomas is national director.

National Organization for Victim Assistance
717 D Street NW
Washington, DC 20004

NOVA is a private, nonprofit organization of victim and witness assistance practitioners, criminal justice professionals, researchers, former victims, and others committed to the recognition of victim rights. Its purposes are to help pass federal and state legislation and to help change local policy that affects the rights of victims, to help victims, to work with local programs in victim counseling and reparations, and provide an information exchange.

Northeast Colleges and Universities Security Association
University of Pittsburg/Bradford
300 Campus Drive
Bradford PA 16701-2898
Phone 617-437-2696

NECUSA is the oldest security organization in the United States. It was founded in 1953. Membership includes schools from Maine to Maryland. George J. Barron, director of security and safety

Tactical Response Association
P.O. Box 17354
Salt Lake City, UT 84117
Phone 801-277-1513

TRA is an organization of professionals dedicated to combatting international terrorism. It is composed of law enforcement officers, hostage negotiators, SWAT team members, intelligence officers, and selected private security personnel. Its purpose is to exchange intelligence and information to combat terrorism. To be an active member, you must work with tactical response problems on a daily basis. Associate and team memberships are available. Kim T. Adamson, secretary-treasurer.

INDEX